CONTENTS

editor
THOMAS DEJA
publisher
SEAN WALLACE
art director
JUHA T. LINDROOS

staff columnists
Mort Castle, Gemma Files, Steve Roman
contributing artists
anonymous (76), Russell Dickerson (24), Shikhar Dixit (16, 42)

UNDERWORLDS c/o Thomas Deja, 55-35 Myrtle Avenue, Ridgewood, New York, 11385

Underworlds is published triannually by Underworlds Magazine and printed by Prime Books, Inc. Subscriptions are $15.00 for three issues. Please send checks or money order payable to Sean Wallace to:

PRIME BOOKS
PO Box 36503, Canton, OH 44735

submissions
Send email to underworlds@rn.com. Attachments preferably in either MSWord or text format.

All submissions should be in standard MS Format. The following information must be included in both the cover letter and on the first page of your manuscript: your name, address, contact number and e-mail, word count. A brief bio should be included in your cover letter.

NEXT ISSUE
New fiction from John Maclay, Shikhar Dixit, Spencer Allen, Jeffrey Thomas, Tim Curran and others; James A. Moore get the Sixth Degree; the debut of Karen Carpenter's Shrouded Kingdom and more!

fiction

features

cover art by Geoff Priest

ISBN 1-930997-23-X

Printed by LightningSource, ltd., Distribution by Ingram

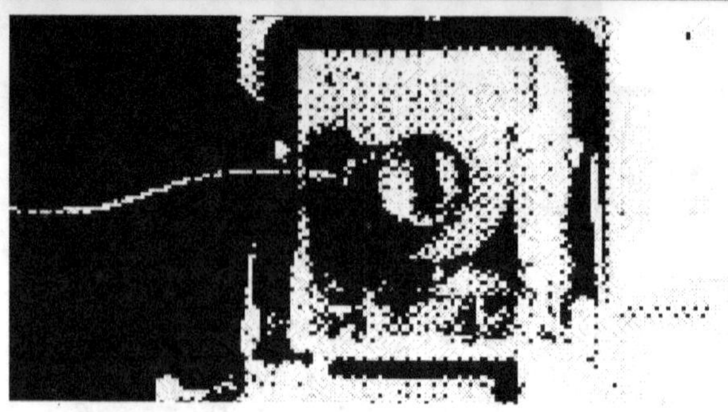

MY DARK PLACES:
MEET YOU AT THE CROSSROADS
By Thomas Deja

Welcome to UNDERWORLDS. I'm your Editor-Pro-Tem, Senor Excellente Thomas Deja.

Within these pages you will find fiction that explores two of my favorite genres, horror and mystery/suspense, and the point where they intersect. And don't get me wrong; these two styles are close relatives, veritable kissing cousins at the very least that have more to do with each other than, let's say, the genre horror tends to be lumped in with usually—namely science fiction.

You see, both horror and mystery deal with the fear of the unknown and how mankind reacts to it. In the case of horror, mankind more often than not falls prey to it and is satisfied with just surviving it. When it comes to mystery, mankind tries to make sense of the unknown, confronting and controlling it by exposing that which is not known to the light of societal truth.

When I began writing far too many years ago, horror was a natural genre for me to explore. I am mentally ill, suffering from a variety of symptoms caused by some neurons misfiring in my brain. If I was one of those that chose to blame my own misfortunes on others, I would point the finger at my natural father, whose abuse of certain substances probably damaged his own chromosomes beyond repair, and whose treatment of myself and my family was so bad that I literally have no memory of most of my childhood. But I'm not one for blame.

Because of my mental condition, I have always felt the outsider. After all, due to misfirings in my brain, my behavior—the general basic operating system that allows me to function in society—is damaged. So it was logical for me to become enthralled with horror, first through the kaiju of Japan thanks to the *ABC 4:30 Movie* here in New York, then later through the fiction of the usual suspects—Poe, King, Lovecraft, Barker.

Oddly enough, because both my parents were mystery fans, I also became easily enthralled by crime fiction. My mother collected Agatha Christie novels religiously, and I discovered *Ellery Queen's Mystery Magazine* in Junior High School. I didn't see these two passions as separate entities guarded by steel walls, neither to cross over and congregate with each other. Quite the opposite—when I would run across Ed Hoch's Simon Ark stories in *EQ*, or discovered the magnificent weirdness of George Chesbro's Mongo books, I knew that mystery and horror were, indeed, two great tastes that taste great together. And I wasn't the only one; when you come down to it, wasn't the overarcing structure of both *Kolchak: The Night Stalker* and *The X-Files* a mystery framework applied to horror subjects?

Which brings us back to *Underworlds*, a magazine built on the prinicple that these two genres belong side-by-side. They even share much of the same lingo, although 'underworld' means different things to the devotees of each genre. My hope is that you those of you who come to me for one of these genres sample the other, or at least give me the benefit of the doubt by reading the handful of tales that bridge the gap—the 'weird crime' stories. And if you like what you see on the other side, I encourage you to seek out works by these authors and explore what's out there.

After I let you go, you'll meet a criminal who finds redemption in protecting the most unlikely of outlaws; a reporter whose search for the most racist mayors in America may end up in a darker part of town; a pair of sisters whose lives are changed irrevocably by a trip to a supposed 'haunted house'; a college student in love with something that brings him to an emotional crossroads in Harlem; and other interesting people in situations you can be grateful you never have to go through. Each one of these characters has some dark places all their own. May you recognize your dark places in theirs.

Enjoy the trip.

Thomas Deja

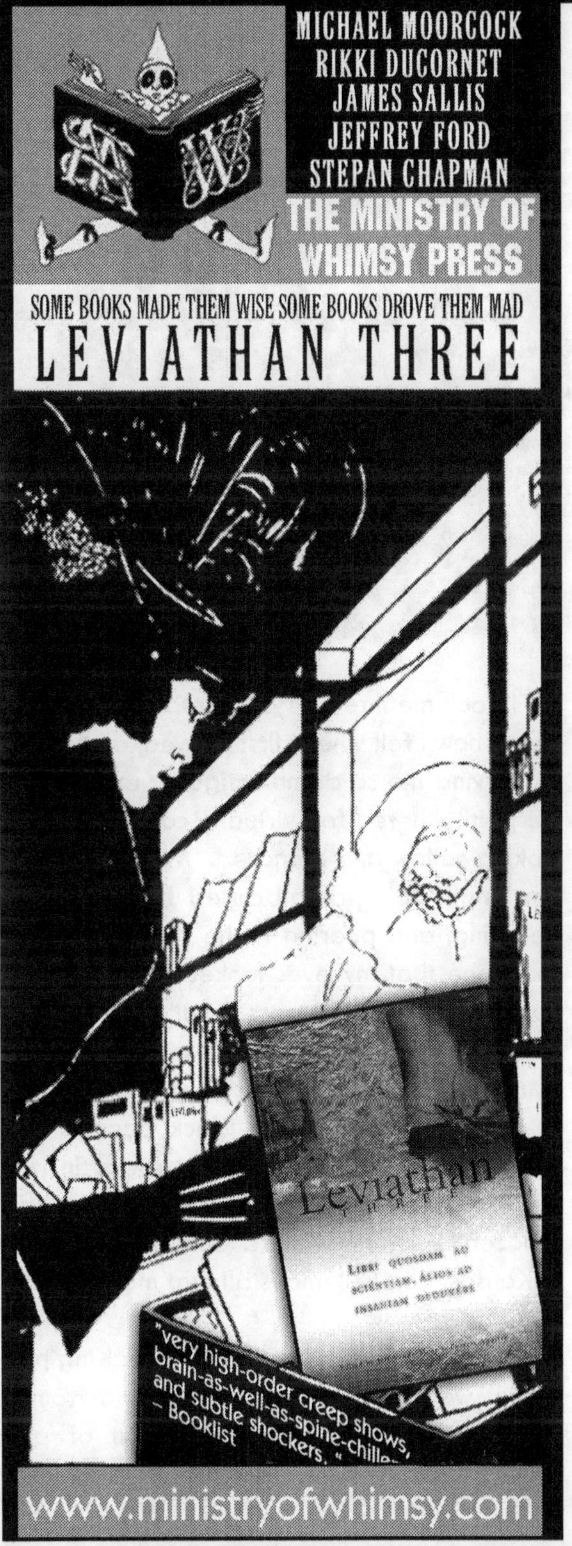

JT LINDROOS

ADMIT ONE Michael Laimo

Five Minutes to Video

Price - $3.00
Tax - .30
TOTAL $3.30

VOID IF DETACHED

It took me three days to get there. I remembered how I felt when I first arrived, all that driving having me so damn fatigued, exhausted to the point where I felt virtually colorless, my skin looking sallow and blanched. My blonde shoulder-length hair was all curled from a want of cleansing, and peering in the rearview mirror I could see that my eyes looked like empty pinpoints beneath my specs. But I really didn't care. Appearance held no importance when you hadn't slept much in three days.

The emergence of my black Camaro stood evidence enough that a stranger was in Hutch Grove. The car was old, its framework rusted by a dozen New York winters. But it had gotten me to Kansas, and hell, that's all that mattered right now.

All eyes in and around the Burger King parking lot were cast on me as I stepped from the driver's seat. I felt hopelessly out of place with my black denims, biker jacket, and military boots, especially in a town that measured your worth by how many pairs of Wrangler jeans you had, or how clean you kept the gun rack on the back of your pick-up.

Fuck it. Out of place or not, I had a good reason to be here.

I was hungry but also needed directions. I strayed into the Burger King and walked up to the only available register. The welcoming smile I received made me think at first that I'd been recognized. It never ceases to amaze me how many people remember me from the talk shows I've appeared on.

"Hello, how can I help you?"

I ordered a burger, fries, and soda. As the young girl gathered my meal, I noticed she carried a slight limp. I wondered if it had anything to do with . . .

She returned, smiling as if life was a bowl of peaches and cream.

"I was wondering . . . could you tell me

where I could buy a map?" I asked.

"Of Kansas?" Her smile went on, as if nothing at all could possibly be wrong.

"No. Hutch Grove." I kept the sentences short. I felt eyes on me and wanted to get back to the car.

Her grin broadened. "Town's not that big."

"How about a hotel?"

"The Hutch Lodge. Just a few minutes up the road, behind the Supermarket."

"Thanks." I hurried back to the car, thinking of her smile that seemed to say, everything's just perfect. I'd believe it if I hadn't already known about Hutch Grove's odd secret. I ate in my car, watching the comings and goings of those choosing Burger King for lunch. An elderly man stopped a few feet from my car and peered at me with one squinting eye. His other eye appeared devoid of sight, the socket slightly smaller than its partner, the eyeball itself a stark crimson, as if gorged with blood. I ignored his glances and he soon moved away.

Fifteen minutes later I pulled into the parking lot of the Hutch Lodge.

The proprietor at the motel seemed normal, so to speak, and as far as I could tell possessed a fair amount of personality and intelligence. I kept the conversation between us brief, limiting it to only necessary pleasantries.

Once in my room I checked my equipment: camera, lenses, video camcorder, flash; everything seemed in working order. I loaded the film, checked out the sound. Fine.

Ready to go.

I'm a photographer by trade, an artist by heart. I started out my career with sculpture, then painting, but soon lost interest—and money. Like an addict needing to increase the dosage, or find a new kind of fix, I felt the urge to move on to something else, something bigger and better. Something more extreme. Photog-

raphy had become the answer for me.

At once my photos started selling, first through ads I placed in underground journals, then mostly over the world wide web. That's when the dough really started rolling in. I charged nine-ninety-five a month, billed by phone or credit card. This would gain you complete access to one of five online libraries: men, women, children, animals, and—don't ask me why—the most popular, babies. I realized quickly that I could make a hell of a living doing this. God bless the internet.

Is this is a form of exploitation? There are many individuals who think so. I like to think of it as `creating awareness'. It exists, it's out there. I've simply made it my job to find it and show it to the world. One talk-show host compared my art to pornography. I don't doubt that there are those sick-minded individuals who get turned on looking at this stuff. I simply argue that in most cases it's the curiosity factor that draws people in. Indeed curiosity is a form of pleasure, but shock value is a form of curiosity as well, just as the mystique of fetish is. They are synonymous with one another.

My initial awareness of Hutch Grove came to me via the internet. One of my `fans' who'd purchased a membership from my website sent an e-mail saying he had a cousin who resided there and learned of a young couple who had two children that would make suitable subjects. He gave me the parents' names, Hank and Evelyn Manners, and their phone number. I called and got Evelyn Manners on the phone. I explained myself and my work. After minimal coercing, I negotiated a fair price, then set a date and time for my arrival. Strangely enough my arrival date was two days before her due date. She was pregnant with her third child, which I found somewhat alarming.

In the weeks that followed I conducted a

great deal of research on Hutch Grove, gathering nearly fifteen years of medical and birth records. In the end, what I found astonished me. If correct, nearly eight percent of Hutch Grove's population would make suitable subjects for my photography. The place was a virtual gold mine. Hutch Grove would make me rich, I hoped.

I left my room at the Hutch Lodge at five o'clock, asked the motel clerk for directions to Wheatly Street. A few minutes later I pulled my Camaro up to the curb at house number 12 and started unloading my gear. It had started raining and the air smelled of freshly cut grass and weeds. I shouldered my equipment and made my way up the center walk.

The house was rundown, dark and unwashed. Dirty plastic toys and shreds of sopping newspaper littered the front lawn, which itself was riddled with squirrel-holes and patches of dead brown crabgrass. Two small windows on either sides of the front door were taped vertically along the edges, hiding age-old gaps, and the gutters ran with rust, one dangling askew from the soffit. The front door was peeling with paint.

I knocked, stooping beneath the overhang of the roof to avoid the rain.

Mrs. Manners answered the door. I knew from our conversation that she had just turned thirty, but her sunken cheeks and hunched posture proved to me that age shouldn't always be calculated through the passing of time. She wore a sleeveless floral housedress, the top two buttons opened to reveal a patch of raspberry skin. Her distended belly pressed against the light fabric, extending it to gross proportions, pulling the hem far above her knees. She had her arms folded, as if afraid her baby would fall out.

"Mrs. Manners?"

"Hi," she said, smiling thinly, shifting her heavy body. "The house is a mess right now. I'm sorry."

I shook my head. "No problem. " I knew to keep cool and calm with my subjects. Most of the time they're not used to people coming around. The slightest bit of discomfort with the situation could send them off the deep end—it's happened a few times. Then I'd have a heck of a time getting my money back. I even had a camera smashed on me once.

She backed away from the door. "Please, come in."

The living room and kitchen, from what I could make of it, looked much like it did outside: toys and magazines scattered about, bits of food and scraps of cloth littering the couch, pieces of foam bursting through the frayed fabric like weird fungi. The air smelled rancid, like vegetables gone to rot. But I knew, it really wasn't vegetables I smelled.

It was them.

Her children.

"They each have their own rooms," she revealed. I followed her down a short hall, watching her strain to keep her bloated body from tipping too far to one side. She hesitated momentarily, grasping her pregnant belly. "Little guy's been kicking of late," she grinned. We passed two closed doors and a messy bathroom before reaching the end of the hall.

"This is Carol's room. My first born."

I'd had all the notes on her kids. Carol, age eight. Eddie, age six. Both affected. I'd asked to see Carol first after she revealed to me that Eddie was far worse off. Save the best for last, I thought tactlessly. Didn't care. It was my job. I had to make it entertaining. Otherwise I'd lose my mind.

Mrs. Manners turned and looked at me with swollen eyes. I could nearly see myself in their glassy reflection. "I know you've paid me already," she said, "and I appreciate it . . . but . . ."

"Yes?"

" . . . but you can turn away if you want. I'll return the money. I'll understand."

The look of horror on her face should have been my ticket out, but I declined. Odd. It seemed as if she were trying to spare me of having to go through with what I traveled so far to do, paid so handsomely for. I reminded myself that I'd seen it all before. That there was nothing to be reluctant about.

For a minute I thought she was going to cry, then she opened the door and I went into Carol's bedroom.

"If you need me, I'll be in the kitchen . . ." Mrs. Manners shut the door behind me.

And I was alone facing Carol.

There are literally hundreds of ways a person could be deformed, starting from the most common shortcomings, such as harelips and limb deficiencies, to more serious conditions as dwarfism, Siamese twins, and progeria. And then there are the genetic horrors, thanatophoric dysplasia, cretinism, and elephantiasis.

I'd thought I'd seen it all. But here was Carol, an eight year old girl who should have been playing hopscotch with other children her age, going to school to learn her multiplication tables and spelling, was instead lying naked on her back in bed with malformations unlike anything I'd ever seen before. I could only stare, chilled and disheartened.

It's hard to decide where to start. She had only stumps for legs, one slightly longer and fatter than the other, each ending about mid-thigh where the skin clumped into a collection of mushroom shapes. She had no arms, and from her shoulders knots of twisted fingernails sprouted. A thick patch of hair covered a heavy

glistening spot where her genitals were, running halfway up her torso like the fur on a cat's belly. And then her face—well thankfully it was normal except for her ears which were smallish and slightly flapped over.

She looked at me, grinned—not a smile nor a frown but a nondescript flattening of the lips, which were quite full and beautiful mind you— then turned away and stared at the stained wall. I placed my gear on the floor, removed my camera and started taking photos, wondering the whole time why on earth this girl's parents would venture additional children when their luck had been so rotten. As a rule, I captured her being from every imaginable angle. I went through a role of thirty-six, then put away the camera and took out the camcorder.

Pictures were a great way of revealing the truth, but nothing could tell a tale like five minutes of video.

Ten minutes later I exited the room. Mrs. Manners met me in the hallway with a glass of water; she must've been reading my mind.

"My husband and I tutor her ourselves," she revealed, carefully sitting at a small worn dinette table in the kitchen, her full belly shaking and jiggling like gelatin. "She can't go to school and none of the teachers will come here. Can't blame them, you know? Carol's the smartest of the two—she's not affected in the head like Eddie—and we feel indebted to her. Yet still, it's so frustrating. I mean, what's teaching her gonna do? She'll never be able to work."

I felt shaken. It was what she said. She's not affected in the head like Eddie. While I was taking pictures of Carol I'd figured all along that I'd had the cream of the crop. The ultimate freak. But no, it got much worse, I remembered now. Especially if you didn't have your wits about you.

"You know," she said. "I sure do appreciate

the money."

"And I appreciate your time." I was anxious now to continue my work, all the time thinking, she's not affected in the head like Eddie.

I rose from the table, camera in hand. Mrs. Manners led me to Eddie's room. The door had deep scratches all over on the lower half, and I wondered if they had a dog. I heard a whimpering inside. I turned to look at Mrs. Manners, to get her approval to enter, but she had walked away. I figured this to be my green light.

I entered.

My eyes came to rest on a crib, and I thought for a moment that I'd had the wrong room, that perhaps this room had been arranged for her expectant arrival. After all, according to Mrs. Manners, Eddie was six years old. But I stayed-transfixed and suddenly nervous.

The room was small, painted a dull shade of blue. The smell here was much worse than that of Carol's room, the source of the odor I'd caught when I first arrived. I thought, how much worse, really, could it really get when you were so fucked up?

I went over and peered into the crib.

It was rough. I'd never seen such a distortion of the human form. The child was the size of a small dog, its limbs—I didn't want to count, but there were more than four—protruding from one side of its torso. Prominent yellow nails poked out from the swelled ends at odd angles. Eddie's head was the size of a grapefruit, if that, and completely hairless, the skin a torrent of wrinkles. Its mouth was no more than a tiny drooling hole where the chin bone should have been.

Even still, the most horrible part were the eyes.

Big, wet, and glistening they were, orbs almost cartoonish in nature and peering up at me in near wonderment—in prayerful contemplation of the stranger that had come into its room.

I stared, dumbfounded, taking in the entire scene: sucking sounds, the eyes rolling away for the briefest moment only to return and recapture me. A slight bodily jostle. Then, repositioning of itself. A stream of flatulence. Limbs twitching. Eyes moving again, looking at me, looking at me, looking at me . . .

I raised my camera and shot two rolls of film.

Hank Manners had returned from work and was home by the time I finished with Eddie. He made a pot of coffee and I drank two cups, speaking with him not of their children but of the apparent rise of birth defects in Hutch Grove over the past fifteen years.

"Must be something in the water," he joked.

We talked mostly of my business from that point on. I tried to explain it away as a form of art but I don't think he bought that route, not as much as the Mrs. did. He grimaced and grumbled when the subject of my selling the photos came up, and I think it bothered him that pictures of his children—they were his children—would be available on the internet for anyone to see. I assured him that any and all details regarding their names and whereabouts would remain anonymous. When push came to shove, all he cared about was the money.

"Why don't you tell him, Hank?"

The voice startled me and I turned to see Mrs. Manners standing in the hallway holding her stomach with both hands. I looked back at

Hank Manners.

He scowled derisively at his wife, a look that I interpreted as, *shut your mouth Evelyn!*

"Tell me what?" Clearly they were hiding something. I had to get it out of them.

"It's the kids," she revealed. Hank slammed a fist on the table. Tears welled in her eyes. "We have to tell him!" she yelled. "It's not fair to us or the children. Or the others."

"What others?" I stood up and stepped halfway between Evelyn and Hank.

"There are others like our children in Hutch Grove."

"Evelyn, damn you . . ." Hank stood, fists white-knuckled against the back of the chair.

"I know about the others," I said, wondering if I had missed something in my research. "Eight percent birth defect rate in Hutch Grove. I know."

Could there be something else? I shuddered. I could see it in her face. There were more secrets. And she was about to unearth them— much to her husband's dismay.

"No," she sobbed, "no you don't." I heard Hank Manners pacing behind me. "Hank, I'm telling him, and you can't stop me . . ." Suddenly the tears poured from her eyes. "There is a high occurrence of birth defects here. But . . ."

I stepped to her, placed a gentle hand on her exposed bicep. "What is it?"

Her saturated gaze met my eyes. "The children, they weren't really born that way. It got worse . . . afterwards."

I pulled my hand away from her arm, as if her words had somehow made her contagious. I understood what she said, but couldn't figure as to what she truly meant. "Afterwards?"

"Evelyn! Enough!" Hank was seething, and I could hear his tempered breaths behind me. I kept my gaze on the woman.

"T-the children," she sobbed, "all got significantly worse after they were born. And to this day they still continue to spoil."

Spoil? Did she say spoil? She said the children were spoiling. In a sick, deranged way, that made sense to me. Now, all of a sudden, I understood.

"And my kids aren't the only ones. It's happening to others as well. Even some adults."

It was here that Mrs. Manners shocked me, blew me away.

She lifted her housedress and showed me the most ghastly sight of the day.

From the ulcerated navel of her pregnant belly wriggled a tiny baby arm. It glistened red, rife with veins, as if not developed enough to possess skin.

From inside Eddie's room I heard a ferocious scratching and pounding against the door. I looked at the gouges in the door then remembered those hideous yellow nails he had . . .

I shuddered, swallowing my gorge, then raised the camcorder, pointed it at Mrs. Manners' stomach, and shot five minutes of video.

One year later . . .

I wait backstage for the announcer's cue. The audience is brimming, the lights forcing a sweat upon my brow. The host is now on stage . . .

" . . . *today's guest comes from New York. His photography is quite disturbing to say the least, and not for the squeamish. Through much controversy he has garnered great accolades from researchers and fans from around the world. His work has been compared to those who have documented the travesties of the Vietnam War, and the overcrowding of inner city crack houses . . .*"

I think back to the horror I experienced in

Hutch Grove, to the Manners family, and how the visit to their home has changed my life, has made a horror out of me . . .

"The photos you are about to see will indeed shock you . . ."

They will be more shocked at what I am to reveal today . . .

"We'll also show you excerpts from a video that we had to censor most of . . ."

I think back to the moment when I met Mrs. Manners in the hallway as I exited Carol's room, she standing there with a glass of water for me. Later, Mr. Manners making coffee, me drinking two cups. And then, what Mr. Manners had said,

so much in jest on the surface, so hidden with truth: must be something in the water.

I gently feel under my shirt. Still there, of course. They will be shocked, all right, with what I reveal.

A small twisted mouth with three gnarled teeth, a knot of skin for a nose, and one horrible staring eye. All surfacing from my stomach.

Please welcome our guest to the show . . .

I remove my shirt and walk out on stage.

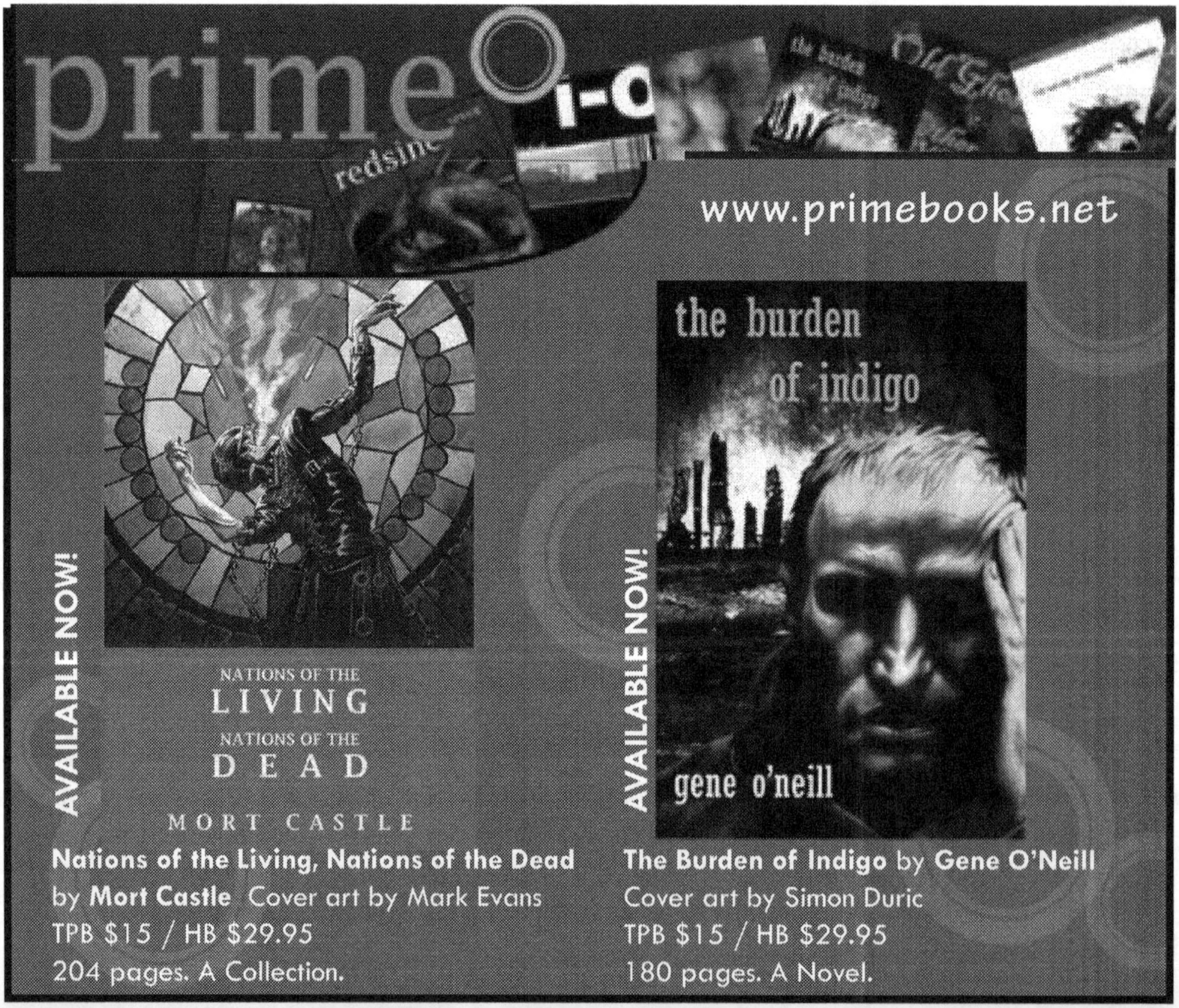

Nations of the Living, Nations of the Dead by **Mort Castle** Cover art by Mark Evans
TPB $15 / HB $29.95
204 pages. A Collection.

The Burden of Indigo by **Gene O'Neill** Cover art by Simon Duric
TPB $15 / HB $29.95
180 pages. A Novel.

MOON OVER HARLEM
Loren MacLeod

The people who know what happened to me say I'm an unsung hero, but since I went to a fancy college I know that's just a cliché. It's true I'm not a bad guy. But I'm not a good guy, either, and I get into these moods where all I can see is a snow-balling chain of events precipitated by Professor Wieland. I mean, I was sitting in the back row of his evening class on ancient astronomy, right? And watching him draw a dramatically simplified version of the Aztec lunar calendar. He was lecturing and muttering to himself as the chalk in his liver-spotted hand screaked around the blackboard, turning my nerves to fried tinsel. Screak, screak. Suddenly, I couldn't tolerate the noises made by my classmates—the coughs muffled, the feet shuffled, the notepapers ruffled. Somebody uncapped a pen—snick!—sending a hot wire up my spine.

It was starting all over again: the clock above the blackboard had frozen, and the overhead lights glared down on the scuffed linoleum floor, the rows of battered wooden desks, and the shiny, blonde hair of my girlfriend, Elisa, who was sitting up front and didn't see me sneaking in twenty minutes late. I was trying to concentrate on the lecture, but ended up fidgeting like a first-grader and staring at the back of Elisa's head, staring at that waterfall of perfect hair. I stared and stared. And then I saw her . . .

face. China's face, that is. China's exquisitely beautiful face. She looked just like the day I first met her, a raven-tressed vision from the Far East in a tight satin cheongsam and high-heeled Corkease, trolling the corner of 125th Street and Broadway with a Newport wedged between her pearly teeth, smiling bemusedly at the wet-smack college kid (me) who had somehow found the balls to talk to her. Now, I want you to understand that Elisa was a really great girl—pretty, sweet-tempered, and smart (a straight-A sophomore at Barnard). But she planned on us getting married right after May graduation and, well, sex with her was like a stubbed toe compared to what China could do for me.

China, my eternal love, fatefully portrayed in the ripples and glows of another girl's hair. She had high cheekbones, a lush mouth, and enormous, almond-shaped eyes that seemed to be all pupil, deep and soft as black velvet. Lustrous, dark-gold skin dusted with what you would think was flour. Or that face powder geishas use. Involuntarily my tongue snaked out of my mouth, wanting to lick it off her.

Screak, screak, screak.

The noise forced me out of the classroom. It was the last straw, tipping me over the edge of restraint. I slipped through the rear door and hurried back to my single in Furnald Hall, where I dumped my books, stuffed the gun into the waistband of my jeans, and pocketed the ten and two twenties I'd stolen from a friend and stashed under my mattress next to the letter from the Dean informing me that my cumulative GPA had rendered me ineligible for graduation. Five minutes later I was travelling, heading north on Amsterdam Avenue.

Columbia's campus sprawls over a hill that crests at 116th Street. By the time I got down to 121st, I'd passed the massive granite walls that rise up on either side of Amsterdam to support the university's fortress of neoclassical buildings. I glanced back once and caught my breath: It was sunset, and the shapes of the towers and temples were imposing against the dying light, which glittered on their windows and set their copper roofs ablaze. But below me waited a trough of darkness: three abandoned blocks of nineteenth-century tenements, gutted by successive fires and slashed over with graffiti, their doorways either boarded up or yawning blackly open like entrances to a tomb. As usual, I got the willies and stepped up my pace. I cursed the string of broken streetlamps that seemed to abet the sinister aspect of those relics. Only a few things could raise the hair on the back of my neck, and that little valley of shadows—painstakingly avoided by even the local hoodlums—was one of them. So you can imagine my relief when I finally reached the corner of 127th and the denizens of the ghetto returned to haunt the crumbling stoops and cratered sidewalks. Steam escaped from mouths and manhole covers, only to be snatched away by the freezing winds that swept down the Avenue and temporarily removed the stench of backed-up drains and food-stamp cooking. I assumed the nasty weather would force most of the criminal elements inside. That way I would only have to watch out for the really strung-out ones, the ones who don't care if it's summer or winter, Tuesday or Friday, 1969 or 1979- just that there's some honky walking alone, after dusk, and they should jump him.

But I had that shiny piece! The nickel-plated .45 I swiped from my Uncle Larry. Prematurely senile Uncle Larry. The NYPD forcibly retired him after twenty years on the beat and took his badge and gun. He bought this one, left it in a drawer, forgot all about it. Now the .45 was a lump of ice pressed against my kidneys, and I hoped it gave me a dick-first, John-Wayne, don't-fuck-with-me swagger. Because in front of the filthy bodegas and ugly red-brick housing projects were guys in flared pants and Shaft jackets, passing a joint or a bottle in a bag, jiving and spitting on the ground and listening to the radio with "Soul Soldier" turned way up. Some knew my face, some didn't. But they all gave me that basilisk stare. I looked up at the sky, ignoring them, and saw a familiar line of cornices and rooftops arranged helter-skelter against a dull-black horizon shot with lurid, flesh-colored clouds. A full moon, as yellow and bloated as a Chinese lantern, floated above a derelict water-tower. I looked back down. Here were vacant lots overgrown with weeds and strewn with rubble. Dark alleyways blocked off by iron gates. Piles of garbage and blackened snow. The ghosts of dead hopes and blighted dreams.

All of which whetted my desire for China.

Minhoi—I affectionately call her "Min," for short—lived in a large but shabby brownstone that had been built in the early 1930s by a successful Negro racketeer to accommodate a migration of relatives from the South. It must have been grand in its day, during the Harlem Renaissance, but now the apartments on the ground floor were knee-deep in trash and reeked of mildew and piss. Disembodied voices floated down the stairs. I bounded up the steps two at a time and knocked the code on 3C, shivering like a dog trying to take a shit in a rainstorm. Come on, come on, come on—

Min opened the door two decades after eternity, smiled, and offered me her right cheek.

"Hello, Chrishtopher." The adorable lisp was courtesy of the gaps in her teeth. A naked bulb screwed into the ceiling above the door turned her skin a ghastly greenish-yellow and shadowed the shallow pits where she had dug into it with ragged fingernails. Her huge eyes were a virtual roadmap of swollen capillaries lacing out from the thin ring of brown surrounding their dime-sized pupils. She was going down fast, her exotic looks losing out to a steady diet of drugs and candy.

Business as usual. I pecked the cheek, and the $50 disappeared into her tiny hand to pay for admission to the shooting gallery, the dose, and the syringe. I'm squeamish, and have an absurdly low tolerance for pain. Min knew to get special rigs for me, namely ultra-thin baby needles laced with lidocaine, stolen from Mount Sinai Pediatrics by junkie nurses and sold to establishments with picky clients like me. These she would place in a cabinet above the stove, away from prying eyes and sticky fingers. I mumbled something about how she should take better care of herself and brushed past her, hurrying into the kitchen, which was an out-and-out horror: sticky parquet floor, stained countertops, and blackened spoons in the sink along with little porcelain dishes scraped clean of every remaining trace of "he-rawn" with an X-Acto knife. And also, in its own corner of Hell, a child's plastic sandbucket overflowing with bloody rigs. I leaned over the grease-encrusted stove, opened the cabinet, and became angry and bewildered to find nothing behind the row of dusty soup cans except . . . hello.

At first I saw just a corner of it, and for some odd reason assumed that it was a gigantic albino cockroach lying belly-up in the shadows. But no, it was brick-shaped and wrapped in thick white paper with a Chinese character stamped on it in bright red ink. I recognized the character at once and knew it wasn't that cheap brown stuff, that Mexican bonita that smells like rotten fruit. No, this was snowy opium powder straight from the misty, dragon-haunted lands of the Orient. This was China White.

Holy Jesus! It came to me, then. A flash of unwelcome insight. Min had a new boyfriend, a coke-snorting, smack-dealing, snappy-dressing, psychopathic hustler called Reggie whose favorite pastime was yo-yoing baby mice in and out of a jar filled with fire ants. This was probably his. Nobody used the kitchen much—that's why the cabinet was such a super hiding place— and I guessed that Reggie had just stashed it in there without saying squat to Min, who, as *tout le monde* knew, could not be trusted with so much as a joint. She, meantime, had obviously forgotten (along with my baby needles) to mention our little arrangement to her paramour.

Now I had the jitters even worse. I mean, man, oh man, where and how does a two-bit thug like Reggie acquire an article of merchandise worth thousands of dollars? But that's as far as I went with that line of inquiry; there was something infinitely more important on my agenda, and I had already concealed her under my coat. The narrow hall was squeezing me toward the back of the railroad apartment, toward the living room, where I saw Min dancing over by the turntable, swaying like a drunken marionette to the Doors while her erect nipples poked through the holes in her macramé hostess gown. Two nodders I didn't recognize were vegetating on the sofa. Winter clothes hid their scarred bodies but not their hands, which were grossly swollen from skin-popping. A chemical smell rolled off of them, as if they were bloated with battery acid and it was leaking out of their pores. Drawing on the surface of the coffee-table was Min's three-year-old daughter, a ghoulish little thing with my nose and the eyes of a circuit-blown robot. Crayolas were scattered hither and thither among melted candles, assorted drug paraphernalia, and a white ceramic statuette of Kuan-Yin, the Chinese goddess of mercy. I glanced at Min again. She had lit another Newport, and was staring up at the cobwebs drooping from the egg-and-dart ceiling moldings, probably reminiscing about the den of iniquity she called home back in Saigon, before she met the U. S. Marine who fell in love with her, brought her all the way back to the States, and dumped her for his high-school sweetheart.

It was a tea-party for the damned, dimly lit. From the bathroom came a stench like a ribbon of foul, pea-green smoke snaking its way through the acid tang of Min's cigarettes. My poor stomach was in knots, but I knew I couldn't risk doing her in the bathroom anyway (the latch on the door was broken). It occurred to me to try one of the bedrooms leading off the hall. I started for the coffee-table and its impressive array of equipment.

"WHERE'S MY FUCKING SHIT."

I jumped out of my hide. Min startled out of her reverie. Twin demons were clattering down the hall toward us—Reggie's two-tone patent Pyramids with the five-inch heels.

"MIN."

I wasn't Min, I was Jack: Jack-be-nimble-Jack-be-quick, and my only choice was to nip into the coat closet, the big one with the slatted wooden doors. I hunkered down on the floor and peered through broken and missing slats. The hems of silk cheongsams caressed my forehead, absorbing the cold sweat that had broken out on my skin. I got the .45 out and shoved its nose into the crack where the doors met. Through the slats I saw Reggie charge in a split second later, volcanically enraged, his gentle green eyes so wide from pumping cocaine that they were about to pop out of their sockets, cartoon-style, and start orbiting his head. Min received a back-handed slap.

"WHERE THE FUCK IS IT BITCH."

Disclaimers tumbled past her rotting teeth. She whimpered and flattened herself against the wall. The nodders bestirred themselves like groggy vampires—Reggie was kicking them in their ulcerated shins. Then he seemed to forget about them and started tossing the place with one hand while the other shakily brandished a gun; I could tell his motor coordination was shot from a powerful combination of anger and fear and blow.

"KILL YOU PIECES A SHIT YOU CUNT!"
Bam, bam, bam.

I jumped and jumped and jumped. As bullets from the .45 blew open the closet doors and exploded into flaking plaster, into the sofa, which puffed up surprised cotton, into Reggie's jerking flesh, and into the soiled shag carpet Min trimmed down with a pair of scissors so nobody would go batshit searching for their pills.

And then, suddenly, it was very, very quiet. For about a minute. Min's record turned soundlessly on its plate. An acrid smell wafted over to me, followed immediately by the overwhelming scent of blood. You should know that the scent of blood does something visceral to a person, that it is nothing you can control. No matter how hard you try to calm your nerves, the physical reactions come.

I knew that someone, somewhere in Harlem—some neighborhood Samaritan—had heard the screams and shots and was going to call the police, and with all the goodies on the premises, I should've split. But no, no, no. I had to cook. So freaked out was I by the noise and the smell of blood that the cops were just a fleeting mental note instantly dismissed into utter oblivion by China. I scuttled out of the closet to grab works off the table, and then I scuttled back in.

Clear liquid bubbled in the teaspoon, absorbed itself into the cotton, and sucked itself up into the pink-tinged syringe. I watched it, shaking with impatience, but had to wait for the ambrosia to cool down (it's that or parboil your heart). Then I raced through the rest of the ancient ritual: tapping the cylinder, tying off my arm with my belt, getting a register, and

. . . you're wondering about China, aren't you? You want me to tell you how she is a sweet, numbing syrup composed of love and desire and knowledge, and that her absence is an insatiable ache in my body, every single cell of which shrieks across the membrane wall, begging for that blessed moment when I sink it home and become a tiny, shimmering being, a gossamer existence twinkling inside a dense opium fog . . .

Well, considering the circumstances, I never bothered to ask or wonder how much the stuff was cut. Sixty percent pure. It hit me like an avalanche. I spent the next three months in a coma, at Mount Sinai, and when I got out I had to stand up before a grand jury deciding whether or not to proceed with an indictment against me on charges of second-degree murder. The state attorneys put up a hell of a case. First, they said I shot Reggie over a drug deal gone bad. But Min, bless her heart, testified to the contrary, and my own lawyers (hired and paid for by my shell-shocked parents) harped about my fine college career and lack of a previous criminal record. Next the state claimed I went into a homicidal rage over her "romance" with him and how he had replaced me as the "father figure" in the life of our child. Min couldn't or wouldn't deny this, so my guys segued into an elaborate song and dance about my happy engagement to Elisa (broken by then, of course) and described my

indifference toward the little girl, whose paternity anyway was mired in doubt due to the sporadic prostitution of her mother. Finally, they claimed, there was the heroic, mitigating, and irrefutable fact that I had saved four whole lives (not including my own) by gunning Reggie down before he went trigger-happy himself. The jury bought it. And that was that.

Other things didn't get wrapped up and disposed of so neatly. For example, the court remanded me to a rehab facility upstate for a healthy chunk of time. And there are still many occasions when I hallucinate and believe that I am glowing like a lantern in the midst of the opium fog. When I turn over in my regulation bed and look up through its darksome layers, I see China. My precious, precious China. My eternal soul-mate. She is magnificent, dazzling, a hundred thousand times more merciful than Kuan-Yin. Her face is a pure and blinding white. Whiter than a skull, whiter than a cold city moon.

the racists
Erik T. Johnson

The oldest and strongest emotion of mankind is fear, and the oldest and strongest kind of fear is fear of the unknown.

—H. P. Lovecraft

The savage black, the ape-resembling beast
Hath held too long his Saturnalian feast.

—H. P. Lovecraft

NIGGER. KIKE. WOP. CHINK. SPIC. TOWEL-HEAD. SAND NIGGER. KIKE. NIGGER. WOP . . .

A. J. Tarot was fed up with hearing these words over and over for the last week. *The ugliest words in existence,* he thought, *but maybe something good will come of this article when I'm done.* He pulled over to the side of the tree-lined road and looked at the map. According to the gas station attendant he talked to three hours ago, he should've passed the waterfall by now, the signal for him to make the next left and follow the road to Gailing.

"Oh, you can't miss it," the gap-toothed grease-monkey had said, more like a wince than a smile strapped across his face, as he leered into the open window of the passenger side of the car.

The map didn't list Gailing or any of these roads around here. It was hard trying to locate these little places with three-digit populations, sometimes near impossible. The sound of a small brass band playing on the fourth of July had led him to take a fork in the road to Trailbait. If not for the wounded tubas moaning he might never have found the dying town. But his article was supposed to be titled: *Small-Minded, Small-Town America: Interviews with Ten Racist Mayors.* A. J. himself found the subtitle a bit much, but the editor of *The Village Cry* insisted that the heavy research implied by conducting ten interviews, and the blatant liberal stereotyping of the little officials, was exactly what their readers wanted. He'd been on this kind of beat before, having

won a prize for an article on girls recruited into the Ku Klux Klan at street-corners in Bensonhurst, Brooklyn. The Klan-Klan Girls.

Trailbait had been the ninth town, the ninth mayor. If he could just get in and out of Gailing he could get back to New York, to the East and to the Left.

Frowning, he put the map down and noticed a copy of *The Forward* on his passenger seat. The headline was about a woman who'd sued her Rabbi and set a legal precedent. A. J. remembered the creepy smile on the gas station attendant as he looked into the car.

"Oh, you can't miss it . . . *Kike,*" was what he'd meant.

His mother was Jewish and A. J. was raised that way. But he looked pure Norwegian, which was how he was able to take this assignment on.

Lost.

That was nothing new on this trip. But he was sure that in this case, the misdirection had been intentional. He may not have enough gas to make it to the nearest town, wherever it might be.

A. J. sat there for a spell and tried to get a radio station that wasn't country or Bible-talk while guessing which way to turn. The faces of the nine racist mayors floated through his mind; they filled the car with their insane babble of "the Negro problem" and "the damn Jews" and "white man's right to the country. " One of them was lean like a man who abstains from food and lives on hate; eight fat-faced and dumb-eyed like monsters made of baby-fat and baby-brains. Just like *The Village Cry* readers would expect.

Tarot heard diesel engines and soon two troop-filled army trucks passed his car, the vague soldiers huddled in the backs showing him itchy trigger-finger eyes as they passed.

Every boy out here's in the ROTC no doubt. The Village Cry would love a piece called ROT, Cunt: The Trials of Women Recruits . . .

There was a red pick-up truck in his rear-view mirror.

A. J. got out of the car and waited. The truck pulled up slowly and stopped. A. J. could hear the radio inside tuned to a country station and the giant American ghost of Hank Williams complained in a small voice:

My bucket's got a hole in it
I can't buy no beer . . .
Here we go, A. J. thought.

The woman who got out wore a T-shirt with a faded Dolly Parton iron-on. Brown roots grew into dyed-blonde, shoulder-length hair. She sported short bangs that sat over big brown eyes lined with too much mascara. Her face, like her body, was round and out of shape. Like many women A. J. saw beyond New York City, she looked a lot like Ozzy Osbourne in his mid-80's phase.

"Hello," A. J. said, smiling genially.

She eyed him up and down.

"Car trouble?"

"Oh, no. I'm lost. I'm looking for Gailing . . . "

She made a face of disbelief, like a friend of A. J. 's once did when he told him a mutual friend died playing Russian roulette.

"Gailing's a hundred miles or so north," she said. "I'm going to New Toomes. If you want to follow me it's twenty miles from here. You could find a phone and call your friend in Gailing, I guess."

"Thank you, I—"

"—Besides," she said, looking around like someone was listening, "you really shouldn't stay around here too long. "

"Why not?"

She looked around once more.

"Black people come through here now and again," she whispered.

"Oh," he said, trying to look frightened or Republican. "Okay. I'll follow you. "

She nodded, got in the truck and started down the road.

"Fucking pig," he said as he got in his car.

Stepping on the gas he threw the black-and-white *Forward* out the window, and it flapped into the trees with the random flight of a wild bird released.

Which is a lot like a reporter chasing down a story.

A. J. Tarot looked friendly; he had frankness in his eyes and his eye-contact was direct and open. He was tall and thin and maybe wore his classic blue jeans and white T-shirts a little too tight, calling attention to his gaunt frame, and on this trip he kept an enamel American flag pin over the left breast of his shirt. He got along well with all types of people. In the nine towns he'd been through on this assignment, not one person responded without warmth to his questions, which were thinly veiled attempts to bring out their racist attitudes.

"You have a wonderfully homogenous community here, mayor," he said in Sirtaut, a town now three hundred miles behind him.

"Proud of it. A real American heritage here," the fat man with the lure-encrusted fisherman's hat beamed.

"That's why I was surprised to notice a colored man drive through earlier. Do any live here and is there any tension as a result?"

A. J. hated saying "colored," but he had to

talk like these people when he was among them. He'd said far worse to fit in with his 'subjects.' It was all the blond haired Norwegian had to do to win their confidence.

"One gets through now and then . . . As long as they keep going, I don't mind it so much . . . Damn coons in their stolen cars," the trout-fisherman frowned.

The mayor of Sirtaut was one of the moderates out here.

"Well sir, my book will be called *The Real Americans: Ten Interviews With The Real Leaders of The Heartland*—and you're surely one of the most down-to-earth of those leaders I've had the pleasure to meet."

The mayor of Sirtaut beamed proudly.

The mayor of New Toomes beamed proudly, too.

"Maggie's led you into town, eh?" he asked. He indicated the female Ozzy Osbourne, who took him to Jack Darn's house when A. J. explained his book to her.

"Yes. Pleased to meet you. I'm A. J. Tarot."

"My pleasure, my pleasure. Tarot— That I-talian?"

"It's a writer's name, actually. I'm Norwegian, given name of Jonssen."

"Writer's name, huh? All right. I'm Jehovah, that's a leader's name."

A. J. wasn't sure how to react when the mayor burst out laughing jovially, holding his sides like the stereotype of a happy fat man.

"I'm Jack Darn," he added with a smile. "Welcome to New Toomes."

Asshole Number Ten.

"I'm writing a book about the real America and its government leaders. New Toomes is about as real America as it gets, and I'd love to interview you," A. J. said, indicating with the sweep of his hand that the old wooden houses and dirt streets were the essence of this great country. All he was missing was the marching band from Trailbait.

The mayor's smile went away in a hurry.

Maggie stood next to her red truck, watching them the whole time like they didn't know she was there.

"Why don't you come into my office?" Darn said.

"Sure. Of course, sir."

A. J. was directed to a back room of the mayor's one-story house. It was an old thing of an indeterminable shade that could've been white, off-white, or a faded yellow or tan. A single long hallway with inscrutable doors set in the walls led directly to the office. There was a large mahogany desk under a window with an American flag on both sides and a golden Apollo 7 replica paperweight. Several animal heads grew from the walls, lots with horns and antlers. A. J. took a red leather seat in front of the desk as Jack Darn sat down pulling on his suspenders.

A. J. noticed *Mein Kampf* on the bookshelf between a volume of *Reader's Digest Condensed Books* and *Jonathan Livingston Seagull*. There was also a book on homemade bombs, *The History of Witchcraft* and *Arthur C. Clarke's Mysterious World*.

"You like to read?" he asked, thinking to draw the racist monster from its padded shell.

"The classics," the mayor replied. "I love the classics. Bible, mostly."

A. J. smiled good-naturedly.

The human on the mayor's side of the desk looked at the human sitting opposite like he was another species altogether.

Sizing me up to be a head on the wall.

"Mr. Tarot, writing's a serious business," he introduced an uncomfortable silence.

"Yessir it is," A. J. finally said. "Especially when it's regarding a serious topic."

He tried to sound earnest and devoted to his craft.

"That's my thoughts exactly. A serious topic. You read my mind, boy."

A. J. laughed a little mask.

"What's this book about, then?" the mayor asked, leaning forward with hands in prayer.

"Well sir, just like I said, it's about the real America. You folks living out here on the unpolluted land of this God-given country."

"And its leaders? You said something before about its leaders."

"Yes. I want to get the insights of the men who have to govern these little, charming towns. What sorts of issues do you deal with on a day-to-day basis? Season to season? How do you run a place like this?"

"The real America," the mayor repeated the phrase.

"The real America."

"Is it authorized then?"

"I'm sorry?"

"Your book; is it authorized . . . by the real America? Did the *real* America okay it? Because the *real* America may not always be what and who you think."

For a split second A. J. actually gave weight to this question.

The mayor interrupted his thought with laughter that broke on him like a water balloon.

"All right then," he said, "I'll talk to you. But there's some things I may not want to talk about. Politics, you understand?"

A. J. didn't understand. Or he did. Or he wasn't sure . . . Jack Darn was a lot more slippery than the other nine mayors were. It was hard to get a handle on him. When he made jokes he seemed to mean them as insults, because of the *schadenfreude* laughter. When he talked on the level his eyes seemed to be on the middle of A. J. 's forehead, as if looking in at

his brain. The mayor seemed way too interested in this part of his guest's face and A. J. shifted uneasily.

"Of course. Whatever you don't want to talk about, we won't, sir. Could you tell me what you wouldn't want to discuss?"

The mayor looked at him with an emotionless chuckle.

"That would be talking about it, now wouldn't it?"

A fucking sophist in the middle of nowhere.

A. J. laughed and smiled and laughed again like a nice person being tickled pink.

"Well, without mentioning it, sir, and with all due respect, it's just that I don't want to say anything you don't want to hear or ask the wrong questions."

A book on bombs. Witchcraft. Nazi propaganda. Typical small-town American mayor.

"Tell me Taro—Jonssen. Are you going to interview anyone but myself?"

"Well if you have a reason I shouldn't I won't."

"Do you think I'm hiding something?"

There was a chameleon on the mayor's mouth taking on the red and white colors of a smile.

"No sir, it's just—"

"—Then answer the question."

"I wasn't going to interview anyone but you," A. J. lied.

Jack Darn sized up the fair stranger. He looked over his shoulder. He even looked under his desk.

"Don't talk to anyone. We don't get visitors much, and I don't want people to start trying to impress you with stories of things that excite them and get them riled up. You understand?"

A. J. did understand. He didn't understand.

"Okay. Yes, sir. I understand."

The interview went much as he imagined it would, with Jack Darn telling of problems with mail delivery and a few spats in local bars, and some road-sign theft by local kids. A. J. was ready to wrap it up and be shown to The Two-Rooms Motel, when he decided to risk a last question. After all, Darn never said what they couldn't talk about.

"What about black people?" he asked the mayor.

The mayor looked over his shoulder and surveyed the room.

I shoot . . .

"WHO DID YOU SPEAK TO?" he demanded in a husky whisper.

"I didn't mean to offend you sir, it's just that Maggie—that's her name, right? Yes, my salvation, Maggie, mentioned to me that there's black people that come by the road back there where she found me lost. I was just wondering if you ever have any problems—"

. . . Score!

"—The Klan are the only ones that understand! God-damn government is a piece of rat-shit when it comes to the matter. God-damn faggots in Washington with their heads up their asses . . . Don't you worry about black people here in New Toomes, Mr. Writer, and don't you print a word of it. Me and the American Knights of the Klan have it all sewed up, you'll see. We got the North Wood Shanties under patrol. If word got out the rat's- assed homos in DC would try to stop it like the leftist pot-smoking hippies that they are. Or what—send in the fucking army? Us and the Knights would run circles round them. And if you should talk, I won't forget your name —I know way more than you might think, Mr. Tarot, like the cards. Hanged-man or Wheel of Fortune, you decide."

Jack Darn laid it out deadly serious. His face grew a bit pink, almost cooked. He eyed A. J. 's forehead with the intensity of a phrenologist.

"I swear I will print nothing of it," A. J. lied with dignity, making the sign of the cross. "I swear on my mother's grave, God rest her soul."

This oath worked like a magical talisman in these parts. A. J. was full of smug confidence. He'd cracked the hardest nut; It appeared his words were good enough for the mayor of New Toomes, who cooled down to a friendly-acquaintance temperature again.

"Well then, God Bless You, Mr. Tarot. The motel is just across the street. Sleep well . . ."

A. J. couldn't. Here he was in town number ten, sitting on what could be the most intriguing story of the whole bigoted journey. He decided he needed to find the North Woods, where there must surely be an African-American community nearby, if that was where the Klan was stalking in shameful sheets under Jack Darn's orders. He needed to speak to the victims.

But first he flipped on the TV with the thoughtless impulse of the typical single New Yorker. Each channel was static, except for Channel Five, which played *Return to Mayberry*. He turned it off.

I might be able to make a real human difference with this article . . . instead of providing the usual masturbation material for righteous New York left-wingers . . . he thought as he got his compass from his knapsack and put on his coat.

The Two-Rooms Motel was just that, with a bed, a dresser, and complimentary lemonade. A. J. left the motel at seven O'clock at night, when the town was quiet and the street was dead. The houses seemed to talk to each other with the pale blue flickerings of television sets through white-curtained windows. A. J. felt he was a child sneaking from a room, crawling through the legs of the adults while they sat together to chat over cake and coffee. He escaped into a star-freckled dark.

The North Woods of New Toomes was a

huge stretch of mostly fir trees that spread up to a tall mountaintop. A pathetic picket fence ran along the perimeter of the wooded area. The fence was three feet high and every few yards a sign was posted in red ink that read: DANGER DO NOT CROSS: THE REAL AMERICA

Das ist verboten.

Easily stepping over the fence, A. J. started into the woods. It smelled sweet and musky and sulfurous and salty, as though here he would find volcanoes and oceans and orchards of decaying fruit side by side. After he'd lost sight of the dimly glowing windows he put his flashlight on and looked for a path. His boots crunched on fir needles and a rotted carpet of black vegetation, while he walked among the invasively surgical reds of false Solomon's fruits, the round blues of huckleberries, and the faded orange of Salmonberries. The further he went the less colors he found, and the world dissolved into bluish black trees and the oily air hanging between them.

Small triangles of moon appeared through the high cathedral vault of leaves, casting uneven tiles of light at A. J. 's feet. Smoky night rolled itself lewdly around him. There was a tension, a touch in the dark air. He took a deep breath and the night seemed to slide into his lungs, and his heart beat faster like a man trapped in a coffin and pounding on the lid. He looked at his hands and found them scarcely distinguishable from the shadowy wind blowing over them.

There was a fast sound that reminded him of newspaper being torn that could've been anything. He thought of his copy of *The Forward* blowing around these backwoods, scaring young Aryan children who might happen to come across it. These ridiculous, sick racists were amazing. They were monsters afraid of the unknown. But there were no more unusual noises, and no burning crosses lighting the woods with hate.

There were no voices at all.

In fact, it grew so quiet he thought he could faintly hear a sitcom laughtrack emanate from town, weird and insanely amused. But as the wind changed direction a moment later, he realized that television sets couldn't be increasing in volume like that: ha ha ha Ha Ha HA HAHAHA-HAHA . . . Or was he just imagining things?

There *were* voices.

A. J. turned off the flashlight and crouched down behind a bloated tree to listen. Cold night wind filled with salt and sulfur now brought barked commands to his ears. The shouting got closer, and someone ran through the trees ahead of it. Someone who couldn't afford to care what he collided with on his way, judging from the sound of branches splintering and pebbles flying.

HAHAHA HA HA HA . . .

The wind died down and the hysterical sound came at him in stereo. There was no doubt he could hear a laughtrack, from the south, in New Toomes. That meant a large group of people was laughing right ahead of him in the murk.

An African-American man burst from the stark-raving woods. As clouds crossed it the flickering moon gave flashes of camouflage pants, army boots and a black jacket, fast as a slide projector gone haywire. An empty holster was at the man's side. A large lightning-shaped gash ran across his face and bled onto fatigues torn in parallel lines as though by a sharpened rake. From where A. J. crouched it appeared the man might've been missing an eye . . . The voices hushed down to dry whispers, but there were shapes in the darkness several yards away, emerging behind the soldier and moving after him in lazy pursuit.

As the man ran toward New Toomes he tripped over a surfacing root and landed on top of A. J. They fell facing each other like lovers on a bed. A. J. smelled piss and shit and blood and sweat and awful toxins he couldn't name.

Both eyes had been torn from the man's head. Night mercifully hid what must've been gouts of blood caked on his cheeks.

The encounter only lasted a second. He yelled and sobbed and gurgled into A. J. 's face, dripping baby nonsense words from a bloated purple mouth. He flipped over like a fish on the docks, rose to his feet, ran into a hard oak, stumbled forward, and found a path through the trees. White things like the tops of mushrooms fell from his hands.

The soldier disappeared behind the inky firs as he ran blindly toward Jack Darn's world.

A. J. rose and retched up those last few seconds of his life. He was thinking with gasoline and his brain was on fire and he was standing in a swamp of sweat but he was full of adrenaline. His heart was a cornered bull raging against his rib cage. This was a real story. This was real fucking journalism. He could pretend to be sympathetic to the Klansmen. He'd successfully infiltrated that group in Bensonhurst and knew how to talk their talk. He would misdirect them, get back to his car and leave New Toomes as soon as he could. Then he would alert state authorities to the atrocities committed in these woods. He could save the blind soldier's life. At least the man wasn't hanging from a broken neck . . . and besides . . .

The article will be Pulitzer-Prize . . .

He only stepped two feet from his hiding spot but felt cliff-diving exhilaration. He turned his flashlight on and pointed it up at his face, as boy scouts do when telling campfire ghost stories.

A. J. stepped on two round, pale glistening things that crunched like they were hollow and wet.

"I'm white!" he yelled out. "Over here, help!

I'M WHITE!"

It was then that A. J. understood that for all his experience in studying the bigots of America, he'd never learned how to *really* crawl inside their minds. Clever as he thought he was, he couldn't think like them. Perhaps it was a credit to his humanity. *Niggers. Moolies. Spooks. Spear-Chuckers. Jungle-bunnies. Negroes. Coloreds . . .* He'd heard African-Americans be disrespected with the most disgusting words in the English language on this trip. But not once had one member of the racist population of this strange America referred to them as Black People.

The moonlight polished the immense ebony horns protruding from the center of their midnight foreheads. They walked claw in claw, swinging long shadowy arms, each one grinning from one mouth, while laughing from another. Robes of dead wrinkled skin hung about them so loosely that small black flakes snowed as they moved. Their thighs scraped together leaving bark-like flesh at their feet. These strips of skin whispered as the creatures following behind crunched them underfoot. Every step they shed layer after layer of oily hide but still they grew larger beneath the fattening moon. That was what A. J. saw before he lost his eyes and the sound of enjoyment enveloped him as a thousand fingers of acid tickled his whole body.

HAHA HA HA HA HA HA HA HA . . .

The whole town was watching *Return to Mayberry* on Channel Five.

SMALL TOWNS IN MAY
DENISE DUMARS

Maitland had been driving through eastern Washington for some time before he came upon the small town called Brenner, pop. 795. He added it up, reduced the numbers to a single digit. An odd number. OK.

The town had come out of nowhere, just appeared when he'd rounded a curve in the road. Rose's Cafe and the Brenner Motor Hotel had appeared first, on the right. Then a hardware store and a bar called Rudy's Roadhouse, on the left.

His turquoise Pontiac matched one of the bands of color in a spectacular sunset as he pulled into the "motor hotel." He got out and was immediately shocked by the bone-chilling cold. His chambray shirt, jeans and denim jacket had been warm enough for Oregon, where cloud cover kept some of the heat in. But here, east of the mountains, the air was bone-dry and cold as hell.

He'd hated Oregon. Too many trees. Too many bushes, too much greenery of all types. You never knew who or what was hiding in those bushes. One town seemed to come after another. Maitland was convinced that one day the suburbs of Seattle would meet the suburbs of El Lay. He hadn't stopped in Oregon at all except to use the rest stop.

It wasn't only the weather in eastern Washington that chilled his bones. He knew he was in a strange place this time—not the imagined strangeness of Oregon, where the sodden trees were hung with parasitic plants that reminded him of something from the movie *Pumpkinhead*. No, anyone who thought the deep South was the hotbed of racism in the You Ess Ay didn't know shit about the great Northwest. He hated racists; hated anyone who felt it was his God-given right to dislike someone else because he was different.

He took a folding brush from his

pocket and brushed his long blond hair till it shone gold before entering the motel. With the hair he might be taken for a hippie in these parts but hell, at least he wasn't black.

The woman behind the desk at the motel looked at him like he was a hot fudge sundae. She was 30ish and kind of heavy—that didn't usually bother Maitland too much—but she also had a double chin, one that seemed to blend in with the slack wattle of her throat. He couldn't stand that on a woman, and yet he couldn't take his eyes off of it. She blushed, mistaking his stare for interest.

Once he'd deposited his suitcase in the room he went back out to the car. He'd go to Rose's for dinner. His right hand itched and he scratched it on the steering wheel cover while he drove.

It was only five o'clock but Rose's was packed. Folks must eat early around here, he thought, get up early. There were seats at the counter but the crowd made him nervous. He decided to come back later.

As he drove toward the roadhouse he wondered what would be on TV later when he went back to the motel. Seeing what was on TV in different parts of the country was what took the boredom out of the endless string of featureless motels. He wondered what night *Star Trek* was on here. In one town he'd stayed at on a Sunday night he'd been able to watch episodes of all four *Star Trek* shows—everything from *classic Trek* up through *Voyager*. Now that was something. Maitland even entertained the notion of going to one of those conventions— meet that Marina Sirtis, now there was a babe, even if she was a brunette. But that would mean going to a large city and spending some time there. And that wouldn't do at all, not at all.

Once in a small town in Kansas he'd gone to a drive-in theatre, surely one of the last ones in operation. They'd been showing a Herschell Gordon Lewis retrospective—all of his great films, including *Blood Feast*, which impressed Maitland greatly, and a little film that scared him shitless called *Two Thousand Maniacs*.

Two Thousand Maniacs was about a small Southern town where the inhabitants snatched up unsuspecting Yankee tourists and did them in, supposedly as payback for what the Union had done to the town during the Civil War. It had scared Maitland so badly he hadn't stopped in any small towns for weeks. Then the scare wore off, and he went back to his old ways, but he was still cautious.

The roadhouse wasn't as crowded as the diner had been. A long-hair who Maitland took to be an Indian sat at the bar staring dolefully at a bottle of Molson and two bikers were playing a lackluster game of pool. The TV blared basketball. Maitland hated sports but he was hungry, so he made up his mind to ignore the TV.

He sat at the bar a couple of barstools down from the Indian. The bartender looked like Wilford Brimley. Maitland had thought the actor stole the show in *John Carpenter's The Thing*.

"What'll it be?" the bartender asked. He sounded sort of like Brimley, too, Maitland thought.

"Cup of coffee," Maitland said. "And a menu."

"Can do," said the barkeep, and pulled a laminated menu out from beneath the bar and set it before Maitland. In three deft strokes he produced a cup of coffee, milk, and sugar.

"'Nother one," said the Indian.

"Wanna slow down, Jack?" the barkeep said.

"Why?" he asked.

"It's only five-fifteen. Night's young."

"Yeah, but I ain't. Not no more," said Jack.

"Quit your bitchin'," said the bartender as though it were all one word.

The Indian named Jack hung his head and

did not respond. Maitland figured he was already halfway to falling off the barstool.

"See anything you like?" The bartender was suddenly in front of Maitland.

"Hamburger, well done, no mayo," he said.

"How 'bout some curly fries with that?"

"Sure," Maitland said.

"Knew a man named Curly once," Jack said suddenly. "He didn't have no hair!" He pounded the bar with a large hand and laughed.

Maitland turned slowly toward him. The Indian faced him, and Maitland was startled by the man's red-rimmed, glittering green eyes. He stared at the Indian, unblinking.

Jack put up his hands in conciliation. "Hey, man, I didn't mean nothin'."

Maitland continued to stare. Jack pulled a cross from beneath his Pendleton. "Look, man, I'm a Christian," he said. "Don't be givin' me the evil eye!"

Maitland turned away, but out of the corner of his eye he caught Jack crossing himself. Damned Indians are spooky as women, he thought. Ran in to trouble with them in Arizona and Oklahoma and damned if it wasn't the same here. His right palm itched so bad he rubbed it furiously on the edge of the bar.

"Fuck me!" One of the bikers suddenly yelled, and the other one laughed. Maitland didn't turn his head but guessed the game of pool was over.

"Gonna play another game, Ace?" the barkeep yelled.

"Naw, headin' out," the biker said, and soon the two were noisily stomping their way out of the roadhouse.

The sizzling burger smelled good, and Maitland tried to focus on the aroma instead of the itch. The curly fries, apparently frozen, crackled like icebergs breaking apart when they were dumped into the hot oil.

The alliterative name of the place lent itself to incessant repetition in Maitland's mind. It didn't help that a neon sign reading "Rudy's Roadhouse" was posted above the bar.

"Are you Rudy?" Maitland asked when the bartender put his food before him.

"I would be the man."

"Kinda slow today."

"Yeah, well it's early," Rudy replied, setting down a bottle of ketchup and a jar of mustard before him.

"Yeah," Maitland said. He carefully spread the mustard over the beef patty, then poured a dollop of ketchup on the bun, spreading it neatly to the edges. He put the burger together and then took a bite.

"That well done enough for you?" Rudy asked.

Maitland hated it when someone asked him about his food when he was in mid-chew. He finished the bite slowly.

"Perfect," he said after he swallowed. Rudy nodded and went back to drying glasses. Maitland noticed that the man's hands were almost never still.

"Got a dead soldier over here," Jack said.

That stopped Rudy. "And I said you need to slow down. I'm not gonna say it again."

On the TV the Blazers were beating the Lakers. The only sport Maitland had ever liked was baseball, and that was because he had enjoyed playing it as a child, when his father was still alive.

Maitland chewed the burger and considered. His father, blond, cool-headed. He missed him. So different from his frequently tearful, just as frequently angry brunette mother. He looked at Rudy, trying to guess what color his iron-grey hair had once been.

"Guess I better go home. Ball-n-chain'll whup me if I'm late for dinner," Jack said.

"Good idea," Rudy said.

Jack put a few carefully considered dollar

bills on the bar and stood up. He shuffled to the door and then stopped and turned.

"You gonna be OK, Rudy?" he asked.

"Now that you're goin' home I am."

Jack shrugged and leaned against the door, opening it slowly against the icy wind.

"And shut the door!" Rudy yelled, but Jack was already gone. "Jesus," he said. "I can't afford the heatin' bill as it is."

This didn't seem to require a reply, so Maitland continued with his dinner until the bites of burger and the fries had been finished evenly.

"More coffee?"

He almost shook his head, but thought better of it, and nodded. The drive had tired him more than he realized, and the food had made him feel sleepy.

"Where you from?" Rudy said as he refilled the cup.

"Los Angeles," Maitland said. It was the only answer he ever gave.

"Don't sound like it. I'd peg you as from the Midwest."

"My mother's from the Midwest," he said.

"Ah," Rudy said, nodding as if that explained it.

Maitland wished that just this once he could relax, could stop the counting. One, two, three, four, five. That was the count so far as he could tell right now, but things could change of course at any minute.

He'd wanted to stop the count so many times before, and sometimes had even succeeded. One time in Las Vegas he'd managed to defeat it by simply counting impossibly high, thereby not trusting himself to get an accurate count that would reduce down to the correct digit. He did it by scanning the slot machines, adding up the numbers on the sides of each and counting every one that was occupied. Then he went back to his room and did nothing but watch movies, order room service, and play with the numbers in his count for three days. He could go back to Las Vegas; the weather there was nice this time of year, not like here.

"It always this cold in May?" he asked Rudy.

"No, sometimes it's colder."

"When does summer come in?"

"'Round September," he laughed. "Then winter starts in October."

Maitland pulled out his wallet and placed a ten on the bar. "Keep the change," he said, and got up.

"Thanks," said Rudy.

Then the door opened.

A man and a woman entered the roadhouse.

Two more, Maitland thought. Damn.

As he pulled into the motel he was relieved to see that there were no other cars in the parking lot but the rusted Duster that he assumed belonged to the check-in girl. In his room he carefully laid out his suitcase: the lotions that relieved the itch had not leaked onto his clean clothes, he noted happily. As quickly as he had packed it was a wonder they hadn't. No point in unpacking now; there was no time. No, the Indian had seen to that.

He took out the filleting knife and the shears, then thought better and put the shears back. The gun he took out and stuck in the waistband of his jeans in the small of his back, just like on TV. It wasn't comfortable, but it didn't show under a jacket, and he assumed that was why they always did it that way.

The girl smiled when he walked into the office, and her smile had hardly had time to fade when he put the snub-nosed barrel against her forehead and fired. He turned the key in the cash register and took just the larger bills while holding his breath so he wouldn't have to smell her fouling herself. He dumped the money in the suitcase which went into the trunk of the Pontiac.

He did a quick head count when he reached Rose's. Eleven. Maitland's stomach threatened to let loose of the burger and fries but he persevered, taking the hostess hostage. After she emptied the register and the paying guests were beneath their tables as he had instructed, he pulled out the knife and slid it deftly into her left ear. She made a small "Oh!" of surprise but a scream died in her throat. He made a small circuit of the diner, shooting five customers at random through the tops of the formica tables.

The hostess had been blonde; he was sad about that.

Once he had crossed into Idaho he took off his blond wig and threw it into a muddy ditch. His hand had stopped itching but his bare scalp began to as soon as the cold air seeped into the cab of the Pontiac. He'd have to stop at a motel soon and get out his lotions, but no matter how cold it got he wouldn't cover his head. No, the next place he stayed would need to see him as a bald man.

He took the count again. 232. Add it up and reduce it: still an odd number. Good. He didn't count the Indian. He never counted any of them that he had stared into, as without witnessing their deaths he could never be sure that the aneurysm would be fatal. Besides, it was all too easy that way. A man should have the guts to kill "mano a mano," as they say, without the aid of superior genetics. A gun or a knife. It made him feel humble.

He thought about Rudy and made a mental note to check the listings when he got to the next small town to see if *The Thing* was playing on any of the local channels. He scratched behind his left ear thoughtfully, the reassuring image of Wilford Brimley in his mind.

THE SIXTH DEGREE

It's like the third degree only twice as tough....

in the hotseat SHADE RUPE

A lot of you may not know Shade Rupe, but the man has been around. Never mind that he's got a book of his celebrity interviews, DARK STARS, coming out from Headpress/Critical Vision (where else would you find Teller of Penn and Teller side by side with legendary film madman Alejandro Jodorowksy and Brother Theodore?). Never mind that he self-published FUNERAL PARTY, a fairly transgressive paperback magazine that sought to connect all things dark into a single web of creativity. He's also produced several well-received short films, has had his writings on sexuality published in several languages, and has been featured on the DVD release of The Saragossa Manuscript. He also recently shot footage of WWII-era Polish extermination camps for an upcoming project.

Originally a native of California, Shade has wandered the earth and is not afraid to share his identity, views and opinions with everyone. A taste of his outspokenness is below; you can go to www.shaderupe.com for more.

Shade was asked to choose six numbers from one to one hundred. His choices were then cross-referenced with the master list of one hundred questions compiled by the UNDER-WORLDS Powers That Be. Neither the interviewer or interviewee knew in advance what they'd be discussing. It's interview-as-product-of-the-Id; where else will you hear a noted intellectual champion of identity politics discuss whether he wants to be King Kong or Godzilla?

And now, Shade Rupe gets...THE SIXTH DEGREE!

11. Who would you rather be: King Kong or Godzilla?

Bambi.

33. Describe your work routine.

Wake up. Turn on computer. Check email. Groan about all the junk email I have to delete. Groan about the bad email joke forwards I have to wade through.

Groan about the mailing lists where everyone copies the previous email endlessly. Groan about how much email I have to answer (even though I love to get email).

Open something I'm working on. Write a sentence. Check a few things on google. Get psyched about a new direction from something I've just read on a webpage. Write a page. Sit back. Get some water, turn on the coffee. Look at the clock and realize I have to shower soon and how much it sucks to have to go to a day job, even though the job is fine. Write a half page. Like it. Check something on google. Get psyched. Check email, get good news or a cool forward. Get really psyched. Drink coffee. Realize I have 40 minutes to get to work and I haven't showered. Write a couple incredible emails chock-full of humor and wisdom that I should probably save for posterity. Realize I have 30 minutes to get to work. Wish I could sit and write more. Depending on what I'm working on either email it to myself to work on at work or grab a book or something I'm review-

➡ in the hotseat SHADE RUPE

ing and jump in the shower.

Grab my bagel, orange juice, wait for the train, get to work, check email, download what I'm working on, and work in-between jobs.

57. What should an artist assume about his audience?

That they care about horror. That they are fans. That they want to see something cool. That they're not stupid retards who need to have everything explained to them. That they watch movies. That they rent horror movies. That they go out of their way to see a movie. That they want to be scared, creeped out, freaked out.

59. Are you happy with the state of the genre today?

I'm happy that cool stuff keeps coming out, I'm saddened at how much holding back there is. In the early '80s it was easy to get psyched about a new film, easy to browse the horror sections at the bookstore. Now we have to do research to find anything, which is okay because there really is quite a bit out there if you look for it. As far as horror movies go, it's pretty sad. I rarely get excited about a new horror film that's opening up. Occasionally something will be cool, but rare.

American horror films just aren't creepy anymore. They're jumpy scares. The cat in the cupboard. Occasionally I see something creepy. The new 'The Ring' had some creepy stuff. Also it's sad because the guys who were making the great stuff have been swallowed up by Hollywood and they're just gone. Stuart Gordon's 'Dagon' had some really great stuff going on.

PCism has killed horror. Everyone's even more afraid to be who they are. Writers hold back. Studio executives decide what's frightening. Too many

people have their finger in the pie. Kiyoshi Kurosawa's Pulse has some really creepy stuff going on. No one's seen it. Smaller films have a hard time finding a home. Takashi Miike has earned somewhat of a reputation and we can see a few of his films, but as far as a film being seen on a mass scale ... it's just rare.

There's going to have to be another swing to create a healthy horror industry. People are going to have to relax and not freak out so much. If a child gets killed, that creeps people out. So be it. But today even horror filmmakers and writers find they have to pull themselves back, or they 'should' pull themselves back so they don't 'offend' anyone.

'The Exorcist' would not be made today. It wouldn't happen. Strange little movies are just hard to release because they must return so much money. David Cronenberg's films would never see a projector lamp.

There's an occasional film that will peek out of the mess, but for now we have to look abroad with our multi-region DVD players to find the creepy, scary films.

63. What is there too much of in your genre today?

Too many big stars. Too many digital special effects. Too many teens. Too much pop music. Too much pulling back. Too much PCism. Too many people who don't know what scary is. Too many rip-offs. Too much self-reference. Too many people afraid to really say what's in their hearts and on their minds. Too much censorship.

72. What was the Golden Age for your genre?

The Val Lewton Period (1942-1945) and almost anything from the late '60s to the early '80s.

LIGHTS! CAMERA! MORT!
WILL STEPHEN KING RETIRE?
A SELF-INDULGENT MEDITATION ON RATS AND FERRETS

by MORT CASTLE

yesterday he killed the children

yesterday he killed his children

he killed his three children
he murdered them
he murdered his three children he

no   no

yesterday
yesterday he murdered nat and joe and
ellen kate
his three soft skinned children
nat and joe and ellen kate
his milk breath children
ellen kate remarkable eyelashes
joe tip of tongue at
the corner of his mouth as he colored
and nat oh nat his little boy nat

no

yesterday
i killed my children

    That's the possible opening of a story.
    It will be a horror story.
    And I will write it . . . I'm not yet sure when, but I will write it.
    You see, it's a story concept that's been with me for a while, too long a while.
    This is the premise: A man murders his children.
    Here's the gotcha, the Slinky™ twist-o spin: It is then that you, Kind reader and Horror-taster, discover that the children were only imaginary children.
    And then . . . Here's the thingumajiggy on top of the thingumajig: Just when you, Dark Fantasy Fanatic, are breathing that sigh of relief and rightly getting somewhat pissed off at a

"surprise ending," which is considered a contrivance worthy of the Velveeta Cheese Award, that is when you learn that the guy killed these imaginary children to learn 1) if he could force himself to do something so fucking horrible, and 2) just how much their deaths would hurt him.

He learns
could will my self to melt away
to allow the emergence of
a monster

to become
the monster
metamorphosis
      the stuff of art
          and horror

        *****

He learns

it hurt
they could not come back
what you have given life in imagination
and what you kill in imagination is
gone
gone away
forever

dead
    leaving you
        leaving you
  without the strange
sorrowful comfort
    of memory
my children
were gone

    Well, there'll be more to it, of course. I've got the more planned, but you just might read the story, so, spoiler and all that, but you get it . . .

Or maybe you don't.

I've tried to explain it before, this "horror *nostra*" thing in a meta-fictional work called "Dani's Story":

You just make it all up, right? It's all out of your head.

Uh-uh. Out of my head. Yessirree, Bob. Not that much to it, frankly. Think it up and write it down and when you're done, you stop.

The above passage is heavy-laden with irony.

This horror thing, for those of us who take it seriously, whoo, it gets to you.

For damned sure, it gets to me.

Because, to borrow that used and bruised metaphor, to write this stuff, you must journey to the abyss and look long and hard and take extensive notes and come back with . . .

"The horror. The horror. "

(Thanks, Mr. Kurtz, one hell of a tour guide, he.)

You have a fine view of the Abyss right there when you look into the mirror and see that shaky, vulnerable, sometimes fool/sometimes prick/sometimes just a mess, see that way-the-hell-lower-than-angels/born alone/and die alone and always condemned to self *mortal* looking back at you.

Argh, that's where the horror be, matey!

It's sorta an existential thing, you know? It's the recognition that maybe you/we/all of us are more monster than god—or even worse, the distinct possibility that there is no difference between monster and god.

But, you say, isn't it wonderfully uplifting, liberating, even empowering (to use *the* bullshit term of the decade) to get this stuff out of you, to put it on paper and say, "There!" Creation as catharsis!

Artistic catharsis methinks, thinks me, is a goddamned lie. If catharsis comes from transmuting pain/fear/sorrow into art, then Billie Holiday should have been so uckingfay ebullient

she'd have made Richard Simmons look like C. Montgomery Burns.

So why do it, then, why write horror when you could instead choose to write optimistic vignettes for the upcoming *Chicken Soup for a Chicken's Soul* or a novel about a really high tech submarine in a perfect storm that disappears into thin air, or dazzling wit along the lines of *Dave Barry's Greatest Toilet References of All Time*, or . . .

Bill Wantling, long ago friend and mentor and since his fatal cornonary in 1974, a member of the Dead Poets Society (bona fide!) wrote these lines about his poetic calling:

I'd carry a lunch box like everyone else
if only the voices would stop.

He wrote about

a surly rat in
　　　the rhythm of the blood
　　　　　　that gnaws and gnaws the night
　　　　　　away

A rat?

As that fine writer David Morrell recounts it in his story collection, *Black Evening*, his mentor, Philip Klass termed it "a ferret":

You can tell the bad writers from the good because bad writers are motivated by money and ego, whereas good writers practice their craft for the insistent reason that they must be writers, that they have no choice, that something inside them—the ferret—gnaws at their imaginations and the festering pressure has to be released.

And so now, at last, we consider the question posed in the title of this column:

Stephen King has recently hinted he might retire; will he?

Stephen King is a good writer and so, based on the evidence, I choose to answer in true Socratic/shtetl peddler fashion:

Think "rats" and "ferrets": What makes you think he has a choice?

WANTED: FOR CHRISTMAS
PAUL VICTOR WARGELIN

"You've been cheatin'," accused the tinhorn with the protruding tusk-like teeth. "And you ain't gettin' this pot." He pulled the betting pile towards him.

Including Sawbones' pocket watch, with Alice's faded picture still inside.

The former United States Army surgeon glanced down at the full house in his hand. He was not a professional gambler. He didn't know enough about poker to bluff an imaginary high hand, nor could he cheat without getting caught. He had joined the saloon game out of boredom and got lucky. He never would have bet his pocket watch otherwise. It was old and tarnished, but it was still gold and probably worth at least twenty dollars.

He'd already lost Alice twice.

The Watering Hole saloon was a rat warren in a town with no name that boasted only two streets. Aside from drinking and gambling at the Hole, he could've gone to the whorehouse, but the quality of the ladies just made him lose his appetite for sex and supper.

Now he had some neanderthal accusing him of a crime he wasn't smart enough or skilled enough to pull off. He was about to respond when a cacophony of high-pitched voices broke out with "God Rest Ye Merry Gentlemen," reminding Sawbones that it was Christmas Eve.

"You may search my person," he told his gambling opponent. "But I assure you that there are no cards up my sleeves, nor do I wear any of those . . . what are they called . . . hold-outs."

"That fancy city talk don't mean nothin' to me cheater," said the gambler. "Now shut yer hole and git afore I call the law on ya."

Sawbones reached into the pile and snatched his pocket watch, snapping it open and sighing with relief when he saw Alice's photograph still there. "Fine, keep the money."

The gambler rose to his feet and thrust a Bowie knife at Sawbones' chest. "Drop it cheater or I'll skin ya."

He pushed himself away from the table, clenching the watch in his left hand to keep from shaking. "I didn't cheat."

"I warned ya."

Sawbones bent his knees, drew his .50 Barnes Boot pistol from its home and fired. The gambler was thrown back and through the saloon's large window, scattering the carolers like frightened birds, and splattered down into the muddy snow.

"Call me a cheat, will you?" said Sawbones, scooping his winnings from the table.

One of the carolers, a preacher by the look of his attire, was kneeling next to the dead gambler. Sawbones squatted beside him and started rifling through his pockets, finding a few cards from the deck.

"Lousy bastard. And he called me a

cheater."

The preacher grabbed his arm. "You killed this man and over what? Money from a game of cards?" He let go when Sawbones continued searching the dead man. "It's men like you who make life out here so miserable."

"Reverend," said a gray-haired woman standing among the carolers.

"Quiet, Martha," said the man next to her.

"I've seen a lot of debauchery and unwarranted violence since I set up church here, sir," spat the reverend. "And I've seen fit to pray for the lost souls who've wandered through this town as well as those who live here. But never in my entire life have I witnessed a more heinous act, especially on Christmas Eve in front of these children."

The reverend grabbed Sawbones. "But I'm sure Christmas holds no meaning for a murderous sinner like you. And, may God forgive me, there are some sins that cannot be forgiven." He grit his teeth. "You'll be damned in hell before I pray for your soul."

Sawbones thrust the barrel of the Barnes beneath the chin of the reverend. "I already am."

The carolers gasped. Two of the men stepped forward, but the reverend released Sawbones and waved them off.

Before the reverend could speak again, an explosion erupted in the evening sky above them. A ball of orange-red fire streaked away from dissipating light into the forest beyond the town, leaving a comet trail in its wake.

"A shooting star on Christmas Eve," said the reverend. "This is an omen. "

Sawbones jingled his money pouch and grinned.

Traveling along the snow covered grassy plain following the fireball, but preparing to go through the town housing The Watering Hole rather than over it, the twisting wave of ice and snow skipped across the landscape like a dust devil, and blotted out the sky. At the edge of town, the wave dispersed, erupting into a shower of sleet and hail that punched holes in the clapboard buildings' roofs as if God had dropped a box of nails.

When the frozen mist cleared, three pitch colored horses appeared. Flames from their hooves melted the snow as they entered town. Mounted upon them sat three tall, lanky shadows of men. Clad in high-buttoned black dusters and wide rimmed black hats pulled low on their foreheads, each of them had blood red ovals glowing from their faces just beneath the brims of their hats where their eyes should be.

They were the Dark Riders.

Sawbones looked over his shoulder for the posse the reverend swore he would send after him when the gale of snow pummeled into his face. Saddlesore twisted and bucked, almost throwing him loose, but then the wind died, and the snow floated to the ground.

Pulling his coat tighter around him, Sawbones clucked his tongue and the old horse cantered into the forest. He kept his watch in the palm of his hand, with the chain wrapped tight between his fingers. After an hour, he heard no pounding hooves of pursuit, and sagged easier into the saddle.

Then he saw the trench.

It was about ten feet wide and stretched off into the dark distance. The snow piled high on either side made Sawbones think of the parting of the Red Sea. The ground within the canyon of snow looked torn up as if Paul Bunyan had Babe draw a plow through it.

Saddlesore trotted onto the new path without direction from his rider. An orange-red light winked to life further along the trail, illuminating two parallel thin lines like railroad tracks.

Sawbones heard Saddlesore kick something. He twisted around and saw a small blackened box with tatters of bright colored paper and a ribbon on it.

They came upon the remains of a toy drum, a broken riding stick, a doll, a wooden train, then something as large as a boulder.

Sawbones drew in the reins to halt Saddlesore. The boulder was a large sack with smoke curling up from it and flickers of flame dancing in its folds. More toys sat in the bag, broken and smoldering.

Past the sack, the trench veered off to the left where mangled metal and wood kissed a pine tree.

Sawbones dismounted and examined the wreckage.

It was a sleigh. And next to the sleigh was a patch of scarlet snow, which spread in a dotted, jagged line disappearing further into the woods.

Following the trail he came upon a body. Dressed in bright red with black knee-high riding boots, was a fat man with a shaggy white beard.

Sawbones knelt beside him, noting his burned face, bleeding nose, and charred hands. Dark smoke rose from his torn outfit and pirouetted above him. He picked up the red cap with the white trim next to his head and placed his hand on the man's chest.

He choked when the man's large hand wrapped around his throat. Sitting up, he pulled Sawbones close and glared into his eyes.

"Naughty or nice?" he snarled.

"What are you waiting for?"

Marshal Finn McCardle massaged his temples to keep his skull from splitting open as Reverend Lionel related the story of the murder at The Watering Hole. Eyes clenched shut, he kept his head down and kept his oaths against the Reverend, God, and daylight to himself.

"He shot Tom Conroy in the chest," Lionel said. "Scared the children, and threatened me with that . . . that cannon, then left. No one even tried to stop him."

McCardle ran his fingers along his unshaven cheeks and over his mouth, afraid to open it for fear of telling Lionel to go fuck himself, and then vomiting in his own lap.

"And if you had been doing your job instead of suffering from a night of wanton acts, we'd have that sinner in shackles on his way to the gallows right now."

McCardle stood up. Man of God or not, Lionel was going to get a fist in the face. Then the office door slammed open and a cloud of frosted air rolled into the room like mist.

One after another, three men clad in black greatcoats draping down to their ankles and buttoned up to their noses entered McCardle's office.

"Close the Goddamn door, will ya?" the marshal said, beyond caring about the reverend's presence. The man of God took one look at the strangers and backed away from their advance until he reached the bars of the holding cell.

McCardle stood beside his desk and crossed his arms, squinting at the strangers, and cursing his inability to put them in focus. "Now, what can I do for you boys?"

One of the men closed the door. Another stepped in front of the window overlooking the main street. The third approached McCardle, reaching into his coat, but to the marshal, it appeared as if the man's hand entered a pool of water. The surface of the coat rippled rather than parted.

I must have drunk more than I thought.

He pulled a piece of rolled parchment from inside. McCardle noticed that the man had long thin fingers with sharp arrowhead shaped nails in gloves without fingertips. Each hand had an additional digit.

The six-fingered man held the paper before him and let it unfurl before McCardle's eyes. A word appeared at top: WANTED. It continued to unravel showing a woodcut etching of a laughing, jovial face wearing a cap atop his head, and a long curly beard covering his mouth and chin. Beneath the drawing appeared the name:

KRISTOPHER KRINGLE
and
AKA SAINT NICHOLAS
AKA FATHER CHRISTMAS
AKA SANTA CLAUS
and finally:
DEAD!!

McCardle heard the reverend gasp, glared at him, then turned back to the strange dark man. "What the hell is this? Some kinda joke?" He pulled his sidearm, a Colt . 45 Peacemaker. "Get the hell outta my office 'fore I lock you up you crazy . . . "

That six-fingered claw was around his throat and puncturing his neck before he could blink. His Peacemaker forgotten, he grabbed at the wrist which was as solid as steel and as thick as a double barrel shotgun.

Santa Claus' wanted poster was thrust in his face.

"Have . . . *choke* . . . haven't seen 'im." McCardle managed.

The man let the marshal fall to the floor and turned to Lionel, who sat on the floor, hugging his knees to his chest and whimpering.

The dark man squatted down, pushing the poster at him, then stopped when the reverend held out his crucifix with a trembling hand.

The man recoiled upright with a hiss, reached down to his hip where a long barreled black revolver melted from his coat into his hand.

McCardle scrambled beneath his desk as weapons appeared in the hands of the other two dark men.

The revolvers roared as loud as cannon fire. Lionel contorted under the barrage as dollar coin-sized holes fissured up in his chest, shoulders, thighs, shins, and knees. Then each hole alighted in flame.

As Lionel's body blazed up entirely, McCardle crawled out from hiding to the rifle rack, pulled open the doors and grabbed the Henry rifle, only to forget it was locked in place.

He heard the unmistakable sound of pistol hammers being clicked into place.

Looking over his shoulder, McCardle watched as the three demons, for that's what he now knew them to be, turned in his direction and lifted their arms as one.

And fired.

Sawbones tossed his old army issue blanket over Santa's legs, careful not to touch his bandaged thigh. Propped up against the remains of his sleigh, with his right arm bound in a shoddy sling stripped from the toy bag, Santa blew smoke rings from his corncob pipe.

"You want some jerky?" Sawbones offered, tearing a piece off with his teeth.

"No thank you. I don't eat meat." Santa patted his stomach. "Besides with *this*, I don't think I'll starve. Ho-ho-ho." He reached into a pile containing chocolates, gum drops, and candy canes, scooped up some of the hard candies and plopped them in his mouth. "Ho-ho-ho." He pointed at Sawbones' own girth with the stem of his pipe. "You don't look like you'll starve either. Ho-ho-ho."

Leaving town, the Dark Riders brought their mounts to a halt and lifted their heads at the sound of familiar laughter. Their eyes glowed brighter as they realized their quarry was nearby.

The hooves of their horses flared up, dissolving ice and burning grass as they followed the laugh to a trail gouged through the snow and ground.

Sawbones stopped chewing, and glanced down at his tummy. He felt like an idiot thinking this old man was really Santa Claus.

Old man? Spirit? God?

"I am none of those things," Santa said. "And yet I am all of them."

"Are you him?" Sawbones asked.

"Who do you think I am?"

His cheeks flushed, and he pulled his flask from his coat. "Forget it." Before he could loosen the cap, a snowball crashed into his hand, stinging it with ice. His whiskey disappeared into the snow.

"What the hell do you think you're doing?" Sawbones shouted at Santa, who was packing another snowball in his one good hand.

"Saving our lives."

"In case you've forgotten," Sawbones said, digging around in the snow for his flask, "I have saved your life."

Another snowball crashed against Sawbones' ass, and he fell onto his face in the cold white powder.

"I forget nothing," Santa said.

Sawbones spun around on his hands and knees with an oath on his lips, but Santa had him by the coat before he could utter a syllable. "I know who you are Nicholas Hennessey. A murdering, bitter old jackass with the moral fiber of a coyote in heat. But right now, you're exactly what I need, but you have to be sober."

He let Sawbones go, and gestured at the toy sack. "I'm already behind schedule, and if I don't finish my job, they win."

Santa sighed and glanced up at the moon. "They'll be here soon. They're like bloodhounds."

Sawbones followed his gaze. "Who are they?"

"Children. Unhappy children who grew into bitter men, whose souls were corrupted upon death."

Santa dropped his eyes to his lap, where a charred toy unicorn sat. "Children I've failed." He lifted the unicorn and turned it around in his hand, examining it. "Children whose wishes didn't come true. Children who stopped believing. Children who gave up hope."

Sawbones sneered. "Children who grew up."

Santa dropped the burned toy and broke out in laughter, surprising Sawbones.

"Grew up?" Santa said. "In size yes, but not in wisdom. In gaining responsibility, but not in behaving responsibly. In years, but not in maturity. In ideas, but not in creativity.

"Perhaps I'm to blame. This season was meant to be a time to celebrate life. A time to renew hope and quell fears. A time to be selfless and giving. Instead greed runs rampant. Merchants become richer, and people find loneliness instead of companionship."

Sawbones cleared his throat. "You prefer we all remain children then?"

"Yes," Santa gave a thin smile. "I'd rather see you sharing your toys, instead of killing one another for your possessions. I'd rather see you play in the sun, then slave in unappreciated labor."

"Well then," Sawbones said. "Seeing as how you are Santa Claus, why don't you grant these hombres their wishes now?" He smiled when he saw Santa's eyes widen with understanding. "After all, it is Christmas."

The Dark Riders came to the end of the trench left by Santa's sleigh. The fiery hoof of the leader's horse crushed and burned a small parcel fallen from the toy sack. There was no sign of their prey. Their leader motioned for them to spread out.

Checking the bushes, the Dark Rider once known as Jimmy Parker in life paused as he saw something sticking out from the snow. His eyes widened as he recognized a wooden riding stick with a horse's head. Smooth and shiny, the mane appeared to be made from real horse hair, with a real leather bridle in its mouth.

An emotion intruded upon the Dark Rider's sense of hate as a tear formed from the corner of his eye and the red film covering it began to dissolve. As the tear flowed down his cheek the black skin cracked beneath its watery trail and a light shined through it.

The lead Dark Rider was examining the broken sleigh when he sensed something wrong. He stood up and stared in wonder at a small, naked boy ran through the snow "riding" a horse stick. The other Dark Rider appeared by his side and followed his gaze.

Together, they approached the playing child. On the ground next to the child's prancing feet lay the blackened, smoking skin of a Dark Rider.

The child stopped playing as they stood over him, and glanced down at his feet in embarrassment.

The lead Dark Rider squinted, drew and emptied his revolver into the little boy, who disappeared in a swirl of mist which rose to the heavens.

Jingling music caused the Dark Rider to whirl only to find another naked boy seated cross legged in the snow, cranking a Jack in the Box—his Dark Rider skin disintegrating next to him.

The Dark Rider leveled his revolver at the boy and sent his spirit on its way.

Sawbones launched himself out of the bushes like a cannonball and caught the Dark Rider behind the knees, and they tumbled it into the snow. Raising a syringe he stabbed the demon in the back again and again.

Then Sawbones felt something strike him in the face, knocking him onto his back. The Dark Rider loomed over him, raising a long-barreled revolver.

There was a crack which Sawbones thought was the gun firing, but instead was a whip taking the revolver out of the Dark Rider's grasp.

Santa Claus, battered, bruised and bandaged, retracted the whip back to him. On his hip sat a holstered revolver.

As the Dark Rider turned to face Santa, Sawbones crawled away, hearing the old man say, "You know I can't grant your wish."

Once the Dark Rider was Michael Hand. A timid child whose father beat and sodomized him for six years. Every Christmas, Michael's only wish was for Santa to bury an axe in his sire's head. And every Christmas he was disappointed. He eventually found the courage to kill his father, but by then the damage had already been done. And no late delivered toy was going to save his soul.

"I'm sorry," Santa said.

The Dark Rider remained silent.

Sawbones watched as the black coat of the demon started to ripple and a revolver emerged from it.

Before he could warn Santa, the old man dropped his whip, drew and fired.

The Dark Rider's head snapped back. Its hat few off its head, revealing its black waxen skull and an eyepatch covering its right socket. Shards of skin from its forehead where Santa's bullet struck home drifted down like feathers.

The body crumpled into the snow. As Santa and Sawbones watched, the black covering melted away to show the human man beneath it, which shrunk to that of a child, then faded away, leaving only an imprint in the snow.

"It's done," said Santa. "They're free." He looked at Sawbones. "But you're not, as long as you remain on the path you've chosen." He limped back to his sleigh.

"What are you talking about?" asked Sawbones, reaching out to support Santa's weak leg, then changing his mind.

Santa stopped. "Are you really that dense, or has the alcohol burned out your mind that much?" He tapped Sawbones on the forehead. "You've had a glimpse of your future Nicholas Hennessey. I'd pay it some heed. You've read Dickens, I presume."

With a snap of his fingers, the sleigh was engulfed within a blinding glow and reappeared undamaged, with a new sack of toys in the back. Santa's bandages and sling dissolved from his suit along with his firearm, and his clothes mended themselves. Eight reindeer appeared in the sky and landed beside them.

Sawbones felt his jaw drop. "You could . . . do that this entire time?"

"But of course," Santa said. "You said it yourself, it is Christmas. Ho-ho-ho." He put his hand on Sawbones' shoulder. "You think we crossed paths by accident? By saving me, you've begun to save yourself. You were a doctor once. There's still hope for you, but you've a long way to go before you can escape your fate." He plucked the pocket watch from Sawbones' vest, and clicked it open to see Alice's photograph. "You have to let her go."

Sawbones snatched it back from Santa, who sighed. "She's not yours. She never was. No matter how much revenge you take on those you think wronged you."

Santa climbed into his sleigh. "Wait," Sawbones called out. Santa raised an eyebrow. "Uh . . . I just realized something. We share the same name."

Saint Nicholas shook his head. "Don't remind me." He pulled on the reins with one hand, tossing Sawbones a wrapped gift with the other. "On Dasher, on Dancer . . ."

The reindeer pulled the sleigh around in the trench and trotted back the way Santa crashed landed. Picking up speed, they were in the air before they reached the end of it. Sawbones watched until they disappeared.

He peeled the wrapping from the gift. It was a shiny new liquor flask engraved to: *Nicholas Hennessey. You've reached a crossroads. Choose your path wisely.*

Sawbones unscrewed the cap, lifted the flask in salute. "I could use a good nip right now." He gulped the liquid down, felt his mouth burn, choked, and spat it out.

"Coffee," he mumbled. "Humbug."

BEYOND LEDRA
Cathy Buburuz

As he glided the pirogue through the onyx waters of the swamp, Joel LaBlanc dwelled on the crippling power of his own guilt and its capacity to destroy his peace of mind, his quality of life. He longed for the days when he was able to educe a physical and emotional sense of pleasure, though short-lived, from each slut.

For months now, he'd seen them in dreams, even during daylight hours, dismal images with unearthly voices that beckoned from the bowels of the black bayou, a screaming collage of eyeless faces and bloody torsos bathed in the heady scent of cheap perfume.

A river of booze and blood had not washed away, or even diluted, the after effects of these deeply disturbing episodes. Even here and now, the squalid ladies of the Quarter smiled up at him from the murky waters of the swamp, accusing him with empty eye sockets and broken fingers.

Something splashed in the distance, jolting him back to reality. Probably a catfish or a gator. The Louisiana bayou was a living, breathing thing, day or night. As he lit a smoke to calm his nerves, he wondered if his good friend Dee LaFosse knew his ass from a hole in the ground, and whether or not he had his facts straight about Ledra.

According to Dee, Ledra lived with her daughter in a modest houseboat less than three miles deep into the bayou. Dee said he'd be able to spot it because Ledra always decorated the boat with orange colored lights, candles and jack-o-lanterns to attract the kids. Who'd have guessed a quadroon would participate in something like Halloween. Joel would have thought her time would be better spent summoning the *loa* or gathering the ingredients for *gris-gris*. Maybe she was a little soft in the head. From what Dee had told him, she was definitely more than one crawdad short of a full crate. She had

to be. With her reputation, Ledra could have opened shop in the Quarter, made a killing off the locals and the tourists, lived in luxury forever and a day. Instead she opted for a ramshackle houseboat in the middle of gator country, no better than Joel's own Mama's shack, according to Dee.

He thought about the mysterious Ledra and how he would solicit her services. He had plenty of cash and was a master at manipulation but he worried about how he would explain his needs to her without a confession.

*****

"Tonight it's andouille with red beans and rice, my cher," Ledra announced to Evangeline as she stepped out onto the deck of their houseboat, the spicy aroma of sausage close behind her. "And much beignet for the children." Just moments before, she'd laid out the little square doughnuts covered with powdered sugar to cool on the counter. Later, she'd wrap them in black cellophane and tie them up with lengths of curled orange ribbon.

Ledra took the rocking chair next to her daughter. "The *loa* say someone comes. Do you feel him?"

"Yes, and even though he is too far off to read, it is not a good feeling he brings."

Evangeline felt restless, uncomfortable. She rose up from her chair and gazed out onto the water. Under the light of a pregnant yellow moon, a stranger would assume they were sisters. Though both were lean, hard-bodied and leggy, wrapped in chocolate skin and angelic white dresses, Ledra carried a glint of knowing in her dark eyes that her daughter did not.

Ledra stood beside Evangeline, placed a hand on her daughter's shoulder. "He is confused about how he will approach us and his bewilderment makes him difficult to read. The *loa* say he wants to repent, yet he longs for a time when he will sin again. We will know more soon. For now, let's eat and prepare for the children."

*****

Before he saw the soft twinkling of the lights, he smelled the wonderful scent of smoked sausage. His stomach growled and he wondered if the price of a *gris-gris* would include a meal. He glided the pirogue toward the lights and reached for the rope behind him to tie his canoe to the old wooden post of the houseboat. He hoisted himself up on the deck, careful not to knock over the candles and eerie-faced jack-o-lanterns; his steel-toe boots warned of his arrival, not that it was a surprise anyway. She opened the door before he could knock.

"Come in," Ledra motioned to her daughter, "this is my daughter Evangeline and I am Ledra. We have eaten but you are welcome to a meal, if you want one."

"I'm hungry enough to eat the asshole out of a gator," hesaid with a nervous laugh, despising his choice of words the second they left his mouth. "By the way, I'm Maurice Laveau," he lied. He thought it best not give his real name. "Pleased to make both of your acquaintances."

Ledra watched as the overweight stranger with sausage-like fingers took his place at her table. With grace, she lifted a plate from the cupboard, a fork and a knife from the drawer, and set the table in front of him. Inwardly, she prayed and exchanged thoughts with the *loa* while he made small talk.

"Smells like andouille, my favorite. Just like my dear, sweet mama makes." It was indeed one of his favorite dishes—all that plump and spicy sausage served on a bed of red beans and rice—but he mentioned it only as a false gesture

of friendship, a prop for stimulating conversation in an uncomfortable environment.

The *loa* showed Ledra a vision of this man's mama, a repulsive woman with a black heart, gumbo dripping from the corners of her mouth, clutching a half-cooked crawdad in one hand, a spoon in the other. Secretly, Ledra thanked the *loa* and prayed for more revelations.

"Glad you like it," Ledra said. "You look hungry. Have you come a long way?"

Evangeline watched in silence.

"Naw, not far."

"Trick or treat, trick or treat, give us something good to eat," several children chanted out on the deck. Evangeline lifted the bowl of beignet and left to answer the door. She welcomed an excuse to leave the room. She would spend the rest of this night on the deck passing out treats to the children, hoping the stranger would leave. Besides, she didn't want the children anywhere near this man.

In the absence of her daughter, Ledra made a conscious decision to steer the conversation into the direction of the point. "Why have you come here?" she asked Joel.

"I, um, require your services. A friend of mine told me that you have good *gris-gris* for what ails me." He didn't want to continue. He wanted it to be over. He was uncomfortable in this place, uncomfortable in his own skin.

"Are you sick?" Instinctively, she knew that he was ill and that his sickness was not physical.

"Not really. I just have these bad feelings. Feelings that I've done something wrong. And I probably have, because most people on this godforsaken earth have done bad things. And sometimes I have dreams. Bad ones. I want it all to stop."

Ledra looked past him, into him. The *loa* revealed to her the things alive in his heart. She was sickened by the filth and perversion that dwelled there. All of these things were beyond her, way beyond what she thought possible in a human. Still, she felt no fear of him nor the task at hand. She knew the *loa* would instruct her how to draw the poison out.

She knew he had no formal education, yet she knew he had been taught how to hate, how to manipulate, and even how to kill, by his parents. Through the *loa*, she saw the eyeless faces of his victims, misfortnate prostitutes whose eyes had been gouged out of their heads with a spoon, those poor ladies from the Quarter whose bodies had been dismembered, then tossed to the rapacious alligators of the bayou.

He was here for one reason and one reason only. He wanted Ledra to alleviate the guilt, to erase the haunting images of his victims from his mind. Guilt was a rarity in serial killers but this one suffered immensely from it. Apparently, he'd had a demented awakening, one that led him to believe he could repent then return to his former occupation as a murderer and actually enjoy it the way he used to prior to the onset of guilt.

"Can you help me? I have a lot of money. I can pay you well for the right *gris-gris*." His eyes rolled over the many glass jars that lined her shelves. Surely she had something to rid him of the vivid, disturbing hauntings by his victims, a special little something that would enable him to revel in his kills the way he used to.

She played his game, pretending she did not know exactly why he'd come to her. "Sometimes it is hard to speak of these things that reveal ourselves. Lay your hands, palms up, on the table. Receive the salt and I will know what brought you to me."

Joel did as she instructed, though he worried about whether or not she actually had the power to detect why he'd come. He watched in silent suspense as she sprinkled salt on his palms, then watched her walk to the shelf to select the appropriate jar, just for him. He wasn't sure what the jar held but, to him, it looked like dried leaves. Dull gray-green leaves.

"Evil begets evil," the *loa* whispered to Ledra, "evil begets evil and you must clean him out."

Ledra smiled as she set the water to boil for deadly Oleander tea.

Outside, a gator the size of a canoe, floated lazily nearby.

RISING TIDE

The fingers of Emmett Furst, the sole occupant of St. Dismas Island's tiny jail, waved like nightcrawlers escaping a bucket. A strangled cry emerged from his pinched mouth. The sound sent shivers down Deputy Jake Willkill's back. The noise didn't particularly bother Jake. Thinking about what Emmett had done out there on Alligator Point certainly did, though . . .

Jake looked down at his desk and cracked his knuckles. Why couldn't Emmett have held his taters for the three months it would take for 1939 to roll around? Jake could have retired without ever facing anything worse than the occasional crab man getting hopped up on election whiskey. Emmett had fixed that, though.

Jake shot Emmett a sour glance. Over the years, Jake had lost track of Emmett's many arrests. Emmett's drunken escapades didn't compare with what he had done to heavy-set Mary and bean-pole Catherine Alligood. At least Mary. The islanders had carried what was left of her to the ice-house, where the body would keep until morning. Catherine remained missing, and Jake hadn't extracted one useful word from Emmett. God almighty, what made Emmett do such a thing?

Damn, Emmett didn't even look like he always had. Sure, he still stuttered and smelled of Emmett's eel gut fish bait. But St. Dismasers all had the same pale sunburn and bruise-prone skin, the same loose mouth and dangly ears. Emmett's skin looked more damp-leathery than sunburned. He didn't bruise, no matter how Jake questioned him. His mouth drew up into a tight little 'v', and his ears lay flat against his head. It was almost as if Emmett wore a Halloween mask one day early.

Then there was that other thing. Jake usually listened to *The Chase and Sanborn Hour*. That Charlie McCarthy made Jake's sides hurt from laughing. Tonight, Jake had dialed in late, and on another station. Jake drummed his fingers on his desk and stared at the radio's glowing dial. The announcer interrupted Ramon Raquello's orchestra again. This time it was an announcement from the Secretary of the Interior, who sounded suspiciously like FDR. The voice said something about 'confronting this destructive adversary with a nation united and consecrated to the preservation of human supremacy on this earth'. Then the announcer said that New York City was being evacuated. Jake sighed. He sincerely wished that the county had at least issued him a sidearm.

Jake turned. Emmett sat in his cell as though he waited for something. Jake opened the door and stared out into the night. He won-

LAWRENCE BARKER

dered what Sheriff Lomax was doing, and when and if he would see the Sheriff again.

The sea-breeze, turned cold early this year, froze Jake to the bone. The wind carried the scents of rotten fish and sea wrack, so thick that sometimes Jake thought that he could sink a boathook into the stench. That was not all it carried. Along with the thump and drone of the islanders' makeshift religious gathering, the wind brought the roar of the rising tide. The service, inspired by current events, said that Jake could expect no help from the islanders. The roar said that the sheriff wouldn't reach St. Dismas before the tide changed, if then. Why, the rough sea made St. Dismas as isolated from the Georgia mainland as from Mars . . .

Jake shivered and scoured the sky for falling Martian cylinders. He saw only a crescent moon in a black sky. So what if clouds obscured its top half, so the bottom resembled a silver talon? Omens and signs were the commerce of granny women, not men with a job to do.

A voice sounded from behind him. Jake spun. Emmett stood plastered against the bars. Emmett spat and repeated his words. "Dangerous times are here. Worser ones a-coming."

Jake's eyebrows rose. Emmett hadn't said three words since his arrest, until now. "What was that?"

Emmett laughed. At least Jake thought so. The sound resembled a mule braying inside a whiskey barrel. "Blood runs true, so they say."

"Catherine Alligood's blood?"

Emmett laughed again. If anything, the sound was more grating and unnatural than before. "Never mind that whippet-hound of a whore, nor her lardy sister. You can b-be on the winning side if'n you want. Just like your grandpa."

Jake snarled. Everyone knew that his Grandpa Arnold had left the Army of Tennes-

see in 1864 to join Sherman. Accordingly, Jake had little choice but to grow up a fighter. Jake pulled an oaken blackjack from his desk. He fingered the keys at his waist. "Emmett Furst, you're going to tell me everything that you know. Now." An almost electric charge ran through him as he hefted the club. Jake strode toward the cell. "Where's Catherine Alligood? What did you do with her?"

Emmett nodded toward the radio. "You heard them. The army's losing. The world's our'n. Or will b-be soon enough."

"What? Talk sense."

"Martians have b-been here a long while, watching and learning. Some even p-pass for folks." He ran his wiggling fingers along his ears and mouth. "It's just that now they can take their true forms b-back."

Jake paused. Emmett didn't look quite right. Instinctively, Jake glanced back over his shoulder. He somehow felt even colder. "Damn it, Emmett." Swearing made Jake feel better. "You're about as much of a Martian as Alf Landon."

"Did I say I was? But I will say one thing." Emmett sat down on the cell's bunk bed, leaned back against the cell wall, and crossed his arms. "Didn't you wonder about how easy you collared somebody able to fell the Alligood sisters? Them is strong women. P-powerful strong."

Jake rubbed his chin. It was true that he had overpowered Emmett without breaking a sweat. After Old Man Alligood had died, Jake had seen both round Mary and slender Catherine lift heavy traps more than three quarters full of scuttling crabs.

"Just maybe I let you take me, so we could have this little talk."

Jake shook his head. "I ain't listening to such foolishness."

"Guess you won't never find Old Skinny. Not where I hid her." Emmett rose and turned his back. He whistled a few off-key notes, matching the tune the radio played between announcements. "She was breathing when I left. Wonder how long that'll last?"

Jake silently swore. Catherine Alligood was probably as dead as her sister. But maybe not. She might be alive, somewhere in the canebrake or one of the sea caves. If Emmett had sliced Catherine like he had her sister, Catherine would bleed dry long before Sheriff Lomax arrived.

Jake considered his options. Questioning hadn't done a lick of good. Playing along might. Jake lowered the blackjack. He replaced his angry expression with the most sincere one that he could muster. "What would Martians want with a run-down deputy?"

"More folks than Martians. P-powerful lot more. Even with heat rays, maybe the Martians need help in keeping order."

"Just suppose I cooperated. What would you want me to do?"

Emmett turned back toward Jake. "Take me b-back to 'Gator P-point, where you found me."

"Where you left Catherine?"

"If'n it was, you wouldn't never find her alive." Emmett worked his lips as though chewing tobacco. "Not without help."

"You'll guide me to Catherine?" Emmett nodded agreement. Jake glanced at the radio. If he stayed, he would hear more of the same and feel even more helpless. His fingers rested on the blackjack's smooth surface. Jake nodded. "Alright. I'll do it."

"I thought you might."

For an instant, Jake felt disoriented, like he had guzzled too much of the moon that Old Man Alligood used to make, before the '37 hurricane sank his boat. He closed his eyes and steadied himself on the desk. When they opened, the cell was empty. Emmett stood outside it, so close that Jake could smell Emmett's sour stomach breath.

Jake shook his head to clear it. Somehow, it didn't quite work. The world still looked a little off, as though viewed through a Coke bottle. Jake glanced down at his keys. He had to have released Emmett, and not remembered it. What else was possible?

Emmett motioned toward the door. "'Gator P-point's a long way. Let's get moving. "

Jake glanced from the empty cell, to the dangling keys, to Emmett's oddly changed face. He rubbed his temple in a vain hope that he might somehow right himself. He heaved a sigh. Some things are more important than a deputy with wads of cotton stuffed into his brain. "Catherine Alligood," he reminded Emmett.

"I keep my promises." Emmett grinned. Somehow it reminded Jake of the grin of a barracuda.

Jake crossed the room and clicked the radio off. He made certain that the kerosene lantern had enough fuel for whatever task lay ahead. He lit the lantern and lead Emmett out into the October night.

At first, Jake tried to drag useful information out of Emmett. All he got was foolishness about 'time for the first to wake'. Words became scarcer as the trudge through the canebrake drug on.

Eventually, Jake realized that he was unsure if hours or minutes had passed. Enough leaves hung on to make judging by the sky impossible. What could make something as small as St. Dismas seem so large? Was it the fallen wind-carried leaves that skittered along the ground? The way the katydids mourned summer's death? The way the shadows danced and heaved? Or the occasional green-glowing fox or bobcat eyes that stared from the darkness and then vanished? For all Jake knew, Emmett might be leading him around in circles.

When he and Emmett emerged from the

underbrush, Jake was only mildly surprised to see the moon set over the ocean above Alligator Point. The old, overturned crabbing boat lay in the sea-grass beyond the high tide mark. Pines, stunted by the spray and with wind-twisted branches leaning inward, marked the transition from soil to sand. Pale ghost crabs darted about. In short, Alligator Point looked like it had when Jake had arrested Emmett, even to the dark stain of Mary Alligood's spilled blood.

Jake sat the lantern down and turned to Emmett. Was it just the lantern light and lack of sleep? Or did Emmett really look even more leathery? It didn't really matter. Jake had a job to do. "I've played enough games," he demanded. "Where's Catherine?"

Emmett nodded. "Told you I'd show you. Here I have." Emmett walked to the boat. He removed a rotted board, opening a black pit in the boat's side.

"She couldn't possibly be there. You couldn't have lifted the boat to put her there."

"I've got ways. Didn't you see that b-back at the jail?"

Jake filled his voice with menace. "I want the truth."

"The truth. Looks like you're about to find it, ready or no."

Jake snarled. He took one step toward Emmett, fists balled. Disorientation, twice as bad as before, gripped him. The world rocked and tossed like a crab boat beneath a water spout. Jake staggered. The beach righted itself . . . or at least came close enough for Jake to walk. Emmett gave Jake the lantern. Jake took it and approached the boat. He held up the lantern and looked inside.

Catherine Alligood lay within. Fishing line bound her hands and feet. Rags, torn from her skirt, clogged her mouth. Bruises covered her, as they might any St. Dismaser who had experienced such an ordeal. Jake could see no obvious wounds, although a curve-bladed fishing knife, similar to the one that Emmett had used on Mary, lay beside Catherine.

Jake called Catherine's name. She did not move. For a moment, Jake believed her dead. He pounded on the boat and repeated her name. Catherine's head moved. An incoherent moan escaped her gagged mouth. She opened her eyes and stared up at him.

Jake gasped. The terror in her eyes seemed a whirlpool, ready to swallow him. The beach pitched and heaved beneath his feet, even worse than before. He staggered. The lamp dropped, rolled, and went out.

Somehow, despite the darkness, he could still see her eyes. Pain and horror poured out of them and into Jake. He could not help himself. He threw back his head and screamed out Catherine's agony.

An arm looped around Jake and threw him to the ground. Emmett looked down on him. Fury blazed in Emmett's eyes. Emmett held Jake's blackjack high, ready to crush Jake's skull. Jake struggled as hard as he could. Emmett's grip held.

"Don't know nothing about no Martians." Emmett's voice took on a strange, gravelly quality. "I just know about us Tommorrowers." Jake's struggles grew weaker. He might have given up, except for Catherine's terror. He held on to that like a drowning man held a lifeline.

"What might a Tomorrower b-be? Figure it out for yourself." Emmett leaned over. Beads of sweat dropped from his brow onto Jake's face. "Listen to your radio. Rioting over bread. That Hitler feller. Klan stringing up niggers like they was apples for drying. The more that goes on, the more of us it wakes up. Soon, there'll b-be so many that the whole world will b-be our'n . . ." He threw back his head and gave an owl-wolf cry. "If'n there's Martians, I reckon they'll just b-be more play-pretties for us." Emmett drew back the club, and prepared to bring it down.

A sound of thunder echoed over the beach. The back of Emmett's head exploded. Emmett's eyes rolled back and his jaw dropped. He sat motionless for a moment, and then fell. Jake turned. Sheriff Lomax stood just down the beach. Smoke poured from the barrel of his rifle.

"You alright?" Sheriff Lomax asked.

Jake nodded and sat upright. "You came."

Sheriff Lomax nodded. "As soon as I could. Waters had to go down first." He gestured back toward the mainland with the rifle barrel.

"Besides, folks scared of Martians kept me busy all last night."

Jake's eyes widened. "The Martians . . . what happened?"

Sheriff Lomax snorted. "You believed it too? Well, don't feel too bad. Half the county did." He shook his head and dropped the rifle to a relaxed position. "Wasn't nothing but a radio show. Like *The Shadow* or *Inner Sanctum*."

"A show?" Jake rubbed his head. Sheriff Lomax nodded agreement. Jake motioned toward Emmett's body. "You heard what he said?"

"I heard him talking crazy, about Hitler and the Klan." Sheriff Lomax looked at Emmett and scowled. "More and more folks are acting fool-ish these days. Like the ones what went daft over that show." He shook his head. "It's almost as if a rising tide of insanity were about to swamp us all." Sheriff Lomax came over and helped Jake rise to his feet. "What were you doing out here? Looking for the missing woman?"

Jake motioned toward Emmett. "He prom-ised to lead me to her."

"Did he?"

Jake glanced from Emmett's body, to Sheriff Lomax, to the overturned boat. Jake intended to tell the truth. Instead, the words that emerged were, "No, he didn't. Not a sign of her."

"We'll keep looking." Sheriff Lomax sighed. "I doubt if we'll find her. Too many places to dump a body."

Jake walked over to Emmett and picked up the club. "I can have some fishermen remove Emmett."

Sheriff Lomax nodded and turned to go. Jake followed him. At the edge of the beach, he turned to stare back at the overturned boat. The sun rose above the canebrake. Its fiery light painted the beach a bloody red.

Jake licked his lips. He could practically taste the woman's terror. Something deep within him liked that flavor.

Jake glanced down at his hand. Was it his imagination, or had his skin taken on just a hint of the texture of wet leather? He shook his head. It had to be his imagination. Without him directing them, his fingers closed, as if they gripped the handle of a curve-bladed fishing knife.

Jake turned to Sheriff Lomax. "You really think things will just get worse and worse? Where will it all end?"

Sheriff Lomax shook his head. "I don't know, Jake. I just don't know."

Jake's lips formed a small 'v'. He followed Sheriff Lomax down the beach, thinking of a tune that he had heard Ramon Raquello's orches-tra play last night.

The Celestial Eye

Shikhar Dixit & S. L. Robinson

Little Krissy sat on the porch steps, remembering a bloody vision. The chill autumn breeze sent shivers rocketing through her fragile little body.

It began a few months ago, when Susan, Krissy's elder sister, was thinking about that boy— that boy she wanted to be with. Not be with him like Krissy was with Mom and Susan and Grandpa all the time, but really be *with* him. Susan had swooned on these same porch steps, and Grandpa had gone on pretending not to hear, sucking on his pipe like nothing could be wrong in the world.

Later, Grandpa came to Krissy at bedtime and asked her to "look in" on that boy. Little Krissy had done it then, just "looked in" on him, no biggy-deally, and there she saw him, in his little room with dank, gray brick for walls. She saw him doing things to an animal, some sort of squirrel or something, with a razor. She heard its whimpers in her nightmares for weeks after that, and Grandpa spoke up the very next day. "Susan," he said in his Romanian accent, between puffs at his mahogany pipe, "I don't want you seeing that boy anymore."

Susan had cursed and screamed things, terrible things like, "You're not my father, you can't tell me what to do!" Grandpa didn't flinch from those comments, but Krissy knew they'd hurt him. She just "looked in" on 'ole Grandpa and saw it clear-as-day. And Grandpa looked at Krissy and smiled, because he could feel her sifting around in his head. When it came to Krissy, Grandpa could answer her right back without moving his lips. Krissy was pretty sure that Grandpa could "look in" on other people, too. At least a little bit. Why else would he insist that the boy who tortured animals had a bit of the gift too, when Krissy herself could not see it. "That's what scares me most about the boy," he'd said later on.

Krissy didn't know. And she definitely hadn't wanted another look inside *that* head.

*****

"I want to have sex in a haunted house," Susan announced during lunch. She and the other girls sat on the cafeteria's lawn, sipping sodas and passing around gossip. Now the declaration drew forth a series of gasps, followed by a chorus of, "Who with?"

"Don't know. Didn't think about that. I just want to do it in a dark, scary place…with lots of people around."

"Why with people around?" Cindy asked

bravely.

"'Cause it's more de-lish that way," Susan answered with a decadent gleam to her eye. "Now, let's go back to who with."

"How 'bout with a ghost?"

"Or a vampire."

"Or a big, hairy Werewolf."

"Or Frankenstein."

"How 'bout Bill Clinton," Cindy excitedly added to the list, only to be the focus of appraising stares. She cast her eyes to the ground and started twirling a bright yellow leaf.

"Anyway," Susan continued, "I like the idea of a beast inside me. Wolfman wins."

All heads tilted in thought, each one, Susan guessed, fantasizing about sex—not *one* of them focusing on the horror she envisioned.

*****

Krissy felt Grandpa in her head. She'd been playing with a deck of cards, but put it down to concentrate. He wanted to know what she wanted to be for Halloween.

But I'm already what I want to be.

And what's that, Krissy?

Your little Princess.

Yes, of course you are, Grandpa chuckled—and how that laugh resonated in her little skull—*but for Halloween, you should pretend to be something else. Something you can make a costume for.*

Krissy saw a picture in her head, and though she couldn't tell where it was coming from, it gave her an idea. *How 'bout the moon, Grandpa? Can I be the moon?*

You could be Diana, the moon goddess. Would you want to be the Goddess Diana?

Yeah. That's it! Krissy chirped with pleasure. *A goddess. I wanna' be a goddess.*

You're already my little Goddess.

Krissy giggled. Yeah, she'd be Diana.

Mommy would help cut out a big, silver moon and Grandpa would teach her a little Greek to say, and she could make a gown from Susan's bed sheets. Krissy giggled harder at the thought.

You're very naughty today, aren't you?

Krissy stood and gave Grandpa a hug. He worked so hard to protect his family. Sometimes she saw his past. She would just sit staring into space, daydreaming, and the dream would collide with his vivid history. A young man, handsome, lean, would lead a procession of caravans, automobiles, and sometimes camels. They would cross forests, deserts and frozen tundras. All those romantic sights would make Krissy sigh. Other things, too, but Grandpa could block her probing whenever he wanted to.

Grandpa left all that, the great gypsy life, when Mommy was born, just so she could be safe. Similarly, when the old neighborhood on Jamaica Street in Queens started "going to the dogs," right about when Susan was born, Grandpa moved Mommy and Susan out to "the burbs."

Susan . . . Little Susan, who'd abruptly insisted everybody drop the "little" about a year ago. The year she turned fifteen.

The year she began to bleed.

Grandpa?

Yes?

When do you think Susan will be able to—you know—see?

His brows puckered in some unreadable distress. "I don't know," he said aloud.

"Don't know what?" Mommy asked from behind them. It must have sounded strange to her, Grandpa talking out loud all of the sudden. But then again, he did that all the time. "Don't know about this darn weather," he added detachedly.

*****

"15 Duke Place," Susan said. "Supposedly,

it's got a poltergeist or some shit."

"You're psycho." Cindy shivered.

Susan watched her look at the house. Deep flutes of Corinthian columns flanked the ornate door on the lower level and a massive, second-floor balcony loomed above. Windows sat recessed under sculpted arches on either side of the house, and jutted from the secondary roof that cloaked the balcony from afternoon's sharp sunlight. Atop all this sat another floor, quietly menacing with its eight-foot diameter Rose window, behind which Susan thought she might have seen the curtains stirring. All this gothic silence lay capped by a sloping, gabled roof.

"I don't know about this," Cindy whispered.

"Chickenshit. What don't you know about? You don't know about Lerner holding you while you shiver from fright? He really likes you, y'know."

"Really?" A spark of interest alighted upon her face.

Susan grinned. Cindy was so easy. They were all so easy. Sometimes, it seemed she could look inside their heads, know just what they wanted. That's why she'd taken off her shirt for Tim Lerner. She saw that he'd do anything for her, anything, if she'd just let him feel her up-and maybe later, something more. But Grandpa fucked that up! The sonuvabitch threatened to call the police. It wasn't any secret what Tim did, not to Susan. Animals. Just animals. He didn't do it to people!

But then she caught up with Tim after things had died down a bit. She never let him come around the house, and she buried her thoughts deep (because sometimes it seemed almost as if Grandpa could read them.) Tim, who wrestled Junior Varsity even though he was only a sophomore, now carried Susan's books around school for her, bought her food, makeup, movie tickets, and whatever else she could think of to ask for. She never used a cent of her allowance, just socked it away under the mattress . . . for that rainy day.

I make my own rain, she thought. *And it's everyone else who gets drenched.*

"So whatall are you going to tell *your* mother? She ain't going to let you sleep in a haunted house! And how the hell are you going to get in there?"

"Don't be such a bitch, Cin. First of all, I'm going to be sleeping over your house. My Mom never checks up and yours is just plain obliv-ee-ous! Second, we're going to break in-or rather-Tim's going to break in," she said, mentally adding, *when I tell him what I'll let him do to me if he does.*

The wind picked up auspiciously, lashed Cindy with a passing leaf, and threw Number 15's front yard into chaos. Trees seemed to bend nearly half under the sudden gale. A loose shutter slapped restlessly against the siding.

Glancing up one last time before moving on down the block, Susan thought she caught a blur of motion in the highest window; something like the ruffle of long garments.

*****

Krissy lay on her bed, exhausted from the day. With the night-light burning, the walls reflected a gentle illumination. She luxuriated under her three favorite blankets, her eyes beginning to slide closed.

There's precious little there, Goddess girl.

Huh? Who was that, speaking in her head? The voice was thickly accented, raspy, but its texture was somehow familiar.

Susan's a slut, you know! A whore! A SIMPLE FUCKING WHORE! And you're JUST LIKE HER!

With all her cerebral might, Krissy let out a psychic whopper. It took only a moment for the footsteps to shudder from across the hall, for doors to be flung open as Grandpa stuck his head in. "Baby?"

Jumping off her bed, Krissy darted straight into his arms. Unable to control her own fright, she lost control of her separated modes of speech. "Something spoke to me—," *Grandpa. It's somewhere here. Somewhere near, it's wa—* "tching us, Grandpa. Oh please, what is it!" *What is it!* "What is it!"

"What is it?" Mommy echoed as she staggered into the bedroom. Grandpa had already scooped Krissy up in his arms and turned to Mommy, mouthing "Bad dream." Little Krissy could "hear" him as he simultaneously thought it. "I'll take care of it," he added, louder.

Mommy stroked Krissy's hair and disappeared again.

Grandpa gently set her down again upon the bed. "What did you hear?"

Krissy only shrugged. "I don't know . . . I was trying to talk to Susan and all I got was this—like on the television, Grandpa, when it's really late like on New Years." Last New Year's Eve was the first time Krissy could remember being up so late, until after two o'clock in the morning. Some of the TV stations had turned salt and pepper. They hissed and made no sense.

"Static?"

"Yes. When I tried to get Susan, I got 'stactic.'"

"Sta-tic, honey. Static."

"Sta-tic," Little Krissy repeated.

"And you never got that before?"

Never, she said with the finality of her thoughts.

"Most peculiar. And Susan is over—what is her name, little one?"

"Cindy."

"—Cynthia's house."

"Cindy, Grandpa, and she'll be over there tomorrow night, too."

Grandpa seemed to drop into deep thought. Krissy "looked in" and saw that he wanted to "watch" Susan from now on.

Grandpa shook his head to clear his thoughts. "No, if she caught us, she would be very angry."

"But what if she's in trouble. Grandpa?"

"She'll be fine, Sweety. Now to bed with you, little munchkin," Grandpa growled, tickling Krissy until she couldn't bear it.

Good night, Grandpa.

*****

"You are out of your fucking mind," Tim Lerner said, a smile creeping into the corner of his mouth. The early sunlight of Halloween morning caught his blond hair in a halo. He looked a bit like an angel.

Susan could feel the wetness in her panties. She knew that Cindy next to her was probably feeling a similar excitement. "Am I? Probably. But you'll do it, anyway."

"Why's that?"

Susan stepped up to him, on her tip-toes, and whispered her rehearsed invitation in his ear. The widening of his eyes was barely perceptible, but Susan caught it. *He's good,* she thought. *Experienced.* "Besides, if that ain't enough, you can fuck Cindy here, too."

She could feel Cindy stiffen beside her.

For just a moment, Susan flashed on an image, a picture not from her own mind. Tim eating Susan voraciously as he thrust in and out of Cindy, a paper bag over the latter's face. "Or both of us," Susan added, cinching the deal.

A flash from Cindy's hot brain relayed a similar vision.

I'm getting better at this, Susan thought.

The three stood awkwardly, hands deep in their respective pockets, on Tim's driveway. He wore only a faded pair of jeans and Cindy stole sidelong glances at his chest and the tight pattern of muscles surrounding his bellybutton.

Susan watched the stirring trees behind him, watched for a sign. She put great stock in signs.

Susan. The voice seemed a static-y growl reverberating in her skull. She could not even be certain she'd really heard it. Surprised, she looked up at the sky, searching for a source.

"Susan!" Cindy called again. "Earth to Susan! Seven o' clock, right?"

Susan shook her head. "Right. Seven. Be there, Lerner, or you'll just be missing the best night of your life." She and Cindy walked away, having decided to take the long way home so they could pass 15 Duke Place.

15 Duke Place, whose ornate Rose window bore no small resemblance to Earth's lonely satellite. The moon would be full tonight, she knew. *My celestial eye.*

*****

That night—long after Mom had taken her trick-or-treating in her Goddess outfit—in the tumble of dream-space, Little Krissy viewed a horror show.

Oh God, no! Susan! But her voice could not carry the scream through the murky medium of R. E. M. sleep. Her feet couldn't move, mired as they were in the gook of marshmallowy earth. The leaves, thorny ones with pulsing eyes embedded in their criss-crossing veins, whirled around her naked body—a body that was older in this dream, as old as Susan's.

And the moon laughed down at her, but she was not fooled. She knew who the moon really was.

*****

"Where is that good-fer-nothin' shithead?"

spat an impatient Susan.

"Go easy on him," said Cindy, heavily made-up, boobs spilling out of a short, black dress, "he's probably got performance anxiety or some shit like that."

Susan rolled her eyes, now impatient with Cindy. "You are so *NOT* experienced, Cindy. He's seven*TEEN*, not forty. He's probably had a permanent boner since we cooked this up. If anything, he's just having to walk extra slow or can't remember where to meet us because all the blood's drained from his brain."

Cindy's laughter was cut short by Susan's stony glare. Susan hadn't meant to be funny. She really was uptight about his being late.

"Fuck this," Susan growled. "We can get in there ourselves. We'll worry about the rest later."

Together, they rushed across the street, into the partial shadow of the back porch. Cindy dug through her purse for her mom's expired Platinum Visa card. Susan had asked her to bring it. *Because this haunted house doesn't accept American Express,* she thought. Cindy also pulled a Coleman flashlight from the bag's voluminous confines.

As Susan worked the credit card in the doorjamb, Cindy whined incessantly. Susan agreed with her; she wished Tim were here; she wished Tim were here with a crowbar; she wished Tim were here with a crowbar, shirtless.

"Hold the damn light still!" Susan hissed, cutting Cindy off in mid-whine. The light from the Coleman flashlight was immediately steady.

Click! The back door to the old house swung open a few inches. Susan grabbed the flashlight from Cindy's hands, pushed the door open the rest of the way and walked in as if she owned the place.

With Cindy several feet behind her, Susan rounded the corner out of the kitchen and into the hall-straight into large, hairy arms that held her tight and muffled her scream with a mouthful of fur. With her back against the creature, she could only guess what held her, but a stomp to the foot with her high heel, followed by a half-turn and a knee to the groin, proved her suspicion. She turned as he grunted. "Tim, you son-of-a-bitch! What the hell were you thinking!"

He hit the floor with a solid "umphhh!" and she kicked him again for good measure.

"What the fuck are you doing, huh? This isn't a fucking game! You do what I say when I say it if you want me, otherwise you can get the fuck out."

Tim sucked the air for breath, moaned a bit, and finally spoke. "You didn't have to kick me."

"You scared the shit out of me—"

"I thought it would be a surprise."

"It *was* a fucking surprise," Susan spat, "one I didn't want. " Seeing him squirm in the circle of luminescence cast by her flashlight, she softened and walked over. "Help me, Cin," she said and took his arm. Together they hauled him up. "You gonna' be okay?"

"Yeah."

"Can you still fuck?"

Tim remained silent and Susan could tell he was considering it. "It might hurt, but I really want to." His voice contained an edge of lust. It seemed to have grown deeper.

Susan smiled into the darkness. "Let's go up. I want to find that window."

The flashlight beam glided over the walls, across draped sheets—covering who-knows-what—and across the ornate, wooden bars supporting a banister. "Up here," Susan said, and began to climb.

Tim walked on his own now. Cindy brought up the rear. They reached the landing. Moonlight slithered over the walls, sliding through the windows, Susan guessed, from the house's many front rooms. Or was it streetlight? It didn't

matter. Just the thrill of it all, being in this place where they shouldn't be, made Susan wet. Her groin burned with dull warmth. She knew that soon the wetness would soak through her panties and vent from beneath her short miniskirt. Tim would catch that scent and go wild. Maybe Cindy, too. The girl wasn't likely to admit it, but one night, during the course of a sleepover, she'd locked tongues with Susan. Though she'd pretended to be half-asleep, Susan knew she couldn't have slept through the rest, considering the rapidity with which Susan had lapped at her vagina and made her cum. But there was no point forcing the issue. If Cindy wanted to participate, she could.

They moved haltingly across the second floor—looking in this room or that, all empty—and held tightly to one another. *Was that a figure in the corner,* Susan wondered. No, just a sheet, draped over something else. Did a shadow stir down the hall? No, it was an optical illusion, all this darkness playing on her senses. Susan felt mildly disappointed.

But she had all night to meet a ghost . . . and to fuck Tim into a frenzy. All night.

They wandered up the next staircase, not so close to each other now. They were growing used to the darkness, growing more confident with every step. They were telling themselves that it was all myth, that there were no REAL ghosts, certainly not here on Duke Place. Not here in the neighborhood. Cautiously they sidled their way down the hall, backs hugging the wallpaper so that nothing could sneak up on them.

One more floor to the rose window, Susan told herself. One more flight to creep up.

*****

With the secret tucked inside her, the secret Susan had kept from her for so long, Little Krissy sat by her window, eyes focused on the glowing disc in the sky. She pictured Susan in her mind, and screamed a message at her. Susan must know . . . deep down inside, she must know. She just can't remember.

Krissy let out one psychic whopper after another.

Oh Susan, why didn't you tell anybody?

*****

The fourth floor, in front of the rose window.

Tim has been stripped in a vicious frenzy by Cindy and Susan, Cindy working far more furiously so she could see his penis, grasp it in her cold hand. Tim seemed in a trance, unable to feel his usual disgust for Cindy, forgetting his overmuch lust for Susan.

Susan stripped Cindy. Pulled off her shoes at first, Cindy awkwardly lifting first one foot, then the other. Susan licked Cindy's ankles, pulled at her jeans, fell under the spell of an appetite so powerful that she didn't realize—even as the shadow moved just in her peripherals—that someone, or something, was in the room with them. She tugged at her own clothes, ripping some in the process of their removal, alternately nipping at Cindy's breasts and pulling suction on Tim's engorged penis.

Then Tim turned Cindy over and plunged into her.

Susan locked her mouth against Cindy's breast and slurped and bit for all she was worth.

Tim plunged into her from behind—except that wasn't right. Tim was in front of her. *Tim is fucking Cindy, so who the fuck is inside of me?*

But her mind was raped by desire, drawn into the act so absolutely that she didn't care about the ornate, curved knife, the one that—

—the one that hangs in their living room, in Grandpa's collection. The one Grandpa insists is responsible for all their good fortune, for his long life, for their relative wealth—

—and suddenly her ravaged consciousness shook with phantom screams. Krissy's voice rocketed up and down her spine, triggered electrical fires in her brain, and turned a key in the lock behind which Susan's memories were sealed.

Susan remembered why she was so experienced in the art of sex. She saw Grandpa lulling her into a trance, and straddling her over him, and she knew in that instant that he'd do the same thing to Little Krissy when he got the inkling, because Grandpa just might live forever.

As the hand lunged forward, its trajectory clearly towards Cindy's throat—towards his sacrifice—Susan grabbed his wrist, veered it down sharply, and rammed it into her own midriff.

She heard an agonized scream from behind her. "Nooooo . . ."

*****

Little Krissy heard the scream bounced back down the "tunnel" connecting her to Susan. She saw writhing silhouettes behind a window that looked like the moon.

The house on Duke was his! Though Little Krissy wanted to cry out in despair, she kept her brave face on and "looked in," into the heart of 15 Duke Place. She saw that the only evil in that house belonged to a man.

She also saw that he'd already lost the battle.

*****

Grandpa screamed as his betrayed hand pushed the knife into Susan. Screamed long and hard—his eyes closing in the frustration of his dying spell—and didn't see the figure tackle him, the strong, virile boy who'd been prepared to pleasure both girls. The breaking of their thrall was not part of the plan.

Susan, where she lay dying on the floorboards, could see that. Grandpa had intended only to slaughter the other two, and maybe blank the massacre from Susan's mind later, as he had blanked those other infringements against her childhood. Her death shattered the spell.

Only one final image before the dark embraced her, carried her away from the obsessions that bound her to him—one final image brought her a moment of true delight, brought to her gasping lips, a grin—Tim ramming his sizable fist into Grandpa's face. Then she died. Even the tiny life lodged deep within Susan's belly was no more.

*****

Krissy sent one last whopper as tears flooded her cheeks. One little instruction.

The boy's mind was weak, and he was experienced with a knife. Besides, it was only a matter of time before he did it to a person, anyway.

Tim, she called. *The knife.*

*****

At 15 Duke Place, Tim finished it.

YOU'LL GO BLIND: ONE
Gemma Files

So I was watching DAGON the other day, Stuart (REANIMATOR) Gordon's triumphant return to the regrettably fallow field of successful H. P. Lovecraft cinematic adaptation—it's a version of "The Shadow Over Innsmouth", his classic New England gill-men novella—and I started thinking about horror as Other . . . a time-honored concept ever since the days of H. P. himself, not to mention long before. Yet particularly pertinent now, post-September 11, when a fresh flood of support for the metaphorical demonization of (certain) other cultures can still be occasionally seen permeating our own.

DAGON begins with a vacationing couple, overworked American dweeb Paul Marsh (Ezra Godden) and his sexy Spanish girlfriend Barbara (Raquel Merono), who are touring the coast of Spain on a pleasure-cruiser owned by one of Paul's work buddies. After Paul dreams of encountering a sexy mermaid with very sharp teeth while exploring an enormous, mysterious ruin on the sea-floor, the ship runs aground, and Paul and Barbara are forced to row to the nearby fishing village of Imboca for help.

Imboca, however, proves to be a rainy, cobblestoned place full of incredibly unhelpful people with hyperthyroid eyes, scaly skin and a lurching, shuffling way of walking. The local priest (who has webbed fingers) kidnaps Barbara, and Paul ends up getting the lowdown from town drunk Ezekiel (Francisco Rabal)-apparently, the whole town has converted to the worship of Dagon, "god of all the slimy things of the Sea", and is now populated by creatures caught partway through the process of becoming fully aquatic. They crave human blood, propagate through human women, and their leader-the same gorgeous apparition who haunts Paul's dreams-may hold a secret revealing Paul's predestined connection with this colony of corrupt, heretical horrors . . .

Now available on DVD for sale or rent through Lion's Gate Entertainment, DAGON is a properly atmospheric but fast-paced and surprisingly vicious vision—sexy and bloody without being facile, far more emotionally compelling than its relatively light-hearted beginning would initially suggest, maintaining a continual sense of shrinking options and mounting dread which promises . . . and delivers . . . few compromises on its way to a truly Lovecraftian climax. What I find most interesting about it, however,

is the way that its translation from America to Europe, necessary for reasons of budget and production, has actually highlighted rather than obscured the original themes which provide "Innsmouth"'s lasting kick.

From F. W. Murnau's NOSFERATU on down, the idea of an inherently negative, "degenerate" alien culture infiltrating and contaminating ours from within like an (in)human plague has been one of horror's most enduring tropes. How do we know these people are bad? Because they try to seem like us, but can't, because they aren't: Physically different, religiously and historically separate, mentally and morally distinct. Though they usually somehow manage to find us sexually attractive, not to mention compatible for breeding purposes —the all-too-familiar spectre of miscegenation raising its ugly, half-human head.

I'm not including merely imitative Things From Beyond The Stars like Jack Finney's Pod People in this, mainly because the second part of the Lovecraftian "invader" model is that these aliens inevitably turn out to be part of a far older, stranger universe: Allied with ancient demon/gods like Cthulhu or Shub-Niggurath (the Black Goat of the Woods With a Thousand Young), living proof of forgotten truths, undermining through their mere existence our wishful belief that the world is a bright, well-ordered, inherently sane, fair and positive construction.

Then again, they also usually echo all of Lovecraft's personal pychological tics— an autodidact's fascination with root languages and ethnos-spanning occult symbolism, liberally admixed with a "normal" 1920's-era educated American caucasian's frankly racist fear of genetic contamination and in-breeding. This IS the guy who thought nothing of calling "The Rats In The Walls'" demented protagonist's favorite cat "Nigger-Man" . . . although—in all fairness—a lot of other people wouldn't have either, at the time.

It's a weird combination of appropriation and demonization; on the one hand, this stuff is exotic and strangely attractive, yet on the other, its very attraction might be a Trojan Horse trap designed to lure us into violating the necessarily rigid behavorial standards which help us support our mutual White Man's Burden. Before you know it, the streets of Innsmouth and the world beyond will be jam-packed with bug-eyed hybrids: Human sacrifice, dogs and cats living together, mass hysteria.

By his own admission, Gordon has been trying to complete a version of "Innsmouth" for years. But the project always came to nothing, mainly because no American company was willing to provide the necessary budget for extensive location shooting, underwater photography, convincing makeup F/X and a small but integral dash of CGI. Then Gordon moved to Barcelona, Spain, where he founded the Fantastic Factory film production company-and suddenly, everything became possible.

Already using a Spanish crew, Spanish F/X experts, Spanish character actors, Spanish extras and a sprinkling of Spanish stars, Gordon also decided to concentrate his shoot in the Spanish fishing town of Cambaro, using the native *gallego* dialect as the "secret language" of the Imbocans/Innmouthians . . . a very significant choice indeed, within context. You have to wonder: Attention and financial rewards aside, didn't the native Cambarans resent having their birth-tongue cross-referenced as the cant of a nascent colony of underwater monsters? And better yet, wouldn't H. P. himself have been tickled pink to discover what 1960's radicals would surely call a blatant case of cultural misappropriation at the heart of his favorite ethno-phobic horror fantasia?

(Again, you could easily argue that *gallego* is just the human language used between hybrids and the original townspeople, while the "real" Imbocan language is that trilling, gurgling noise the hybrids are occasionally overheard making amongst themselves-but the irony's a pretty delicious one, nonetheless.)

One way or another, DAGON's a fitting culmination to Gordon's long haul uphill: Another horror classic from one of the few modern filmmakers who really understands Lovecraft "in the original", so to speak. Iaaaaaaa!

Darren Speegle ALONG THE FOOTPATH TO OBLIVION

Night fell like dark honey on the nothing-land and one of the two men under the bridge wanted to know about something.

"Why do we do it, Mace?"

"Why do we do what, James?"

"Why do we kill?"

Mace didn't like the highwayman approach any more than his partner did. "What else is there to do, James?"

"I don't know—work?" He breathed on his glasses, wiped with his soiled teeshirt.

"We did that once. Remember? Let's talk about it over a beer, OK?"

"I want a motel. This time beer comes after. I need new glasses and I smell like blood."

"Fine." Mace knew it was a matter of waiting it out when James got like this.

"I mean it this time, Mace. Shower first."

"Glasses, too? Or can that at least wait till tomorrow?"

James had to admit that he really didn't want to *buy* a pair.

"Some'll come along," Mace said.

They watched a tanker out on the bay for a time. A ghostly moan—extending-into-a-screech sound came from over by the moorings, where one of the hulking captives tried its chains. Otherwise the night was in the grip of calm, the same calm that had settled over the two men. They always knew when they would score. It could be the most desolate, forbidden place, with the chances approaching nil, but that strange prescience was to be trusted.

Sometimes, however, the calm eluded them, and they roamed all night without success. James became hard to live with then, and Mace was not much better. Sometimes James would suggest they simply go to someone's home, do the ecstasy upon them right there, where they had all the comforts of the normals—shower, clean towels and sheets, a refrigerator with beer or yogurt. Mace patiently reminded him how he got, how enthusiastic, how loud, how *inspired* they both got in doing the thing. Oblivion became their only house, and for that reason they stayed out on the fringes, beyond ears more than eyes.

Voices stirred the calm. Two voices, heels on pavement, emerging from the unhardened pitch of night.

The one broke the surface with a confession. "I'm tired of this. Tired of this life, tired of this craving, tired of this disconnection."

"Arnold," said the other. "You need a fix, that's all."

"I hate it when you say that, Buzz. It ain't heroin, you know. It ain't crack. It ain't something you can just buy on the street corner."

"You forget if you think there's that much of a difference. Bottom line is, it's a hunger that screams to be satisfied."

"Don't you remember, Buzz, how it once was? How wide the margin separating this one thrill from all the others? It narrows with every trick."

Mace and James found themselves looking at each other by the thin light from the moorings. Above, the debators drew nearer but weren't yet at the bridge.

"You hate it when I call it a fix, but you never hesitate to call it a trick."

Mace nodded his head.

"Yeah well, Buzz, it's become that cheap."

Now James nodded his.

There was a relatively long pause. Arnold, the raspier voice, broke it. "I wonder, man, you ever thought about performing the trick on me?"

They were on the bridge now. Even the tone of their steps had changed.

"I've thought about it. Especially when you get like this. But then who would I share the thing with? There aren't any others like us, you know. You ever really looked at the expression on Gramps when he gives us the key to our room? I'm sure we're not the only stained shirts to show up at the cheapest, seediest motel in the city, but he looks at us like he's looking at the face of God."

"Faces."

"What?"

"Faces, Buzz. We're two faces not one. I don't care how lost we are."

"It's God that has the one—did you say *lost?*"

Their approach stopped. Mace and James sensed it even before the footfalls were snatched away by night. The highwaymen raised their brows at one another, Mace mouthing the word *Now?*

But James shook his head.

The last spoken word, unlike the sound of the debators' heels, still hung there, almost on top of the highwaymen. *Lost.*

The raspier voice: "What am I seeing in your face, Buzz?"

"*Lost?* As in *souls?* That's bringing religion into it. Never has religion been part of it."

"Is it fear I'm seeing in your face?"

"The blood vessel above my ear is throbbing. Fear is not the emotion."

"Ah. " A pause separated this from his next words. "I've wondered what it would be like . . . at the receiving end."

Night bled with another wailing from the moorings.

"I've wondered if it would be different for one who has visited the act on others."

Silence from the occupant of space to whom he spoke. Silence from the trolls under the bridge, staring at each other, doing a bit of wondering themselves—wondering about the crazy mathematics of chance, about kindred souls on life's crazy roads. It was a more immediate prospect, though, that caused them to moisten their lips with their tongues.

There was a sound like that of air being knocked out of a set of lungs, a grunted exhalation followed by a moment's anticipatory lull. The next was a low, deep moan that gathered strength as it came, stretching into a rolling howl that in turn became something even fiercer, even stranger . . .

The notion of letting the song spread from victim to perpetrator and thereby to fullest blossom before acting was considered and discarded. Never had the two men under the bridge coveted the thing so. In spontaneous union they surged up the short bank, hoisted by the ripping, tearing, screaming stages they knew were on the razor's edge of taking command of the night.

The mouth formed an O as the eyes beheld the deed. The deed faltered only a second as it realized it was under scrutiny—how unimaginative its commencement wound must appear to these experts—then threw itself into its mutilations with all vigor.

He was alone, the perpetrator. Alone, the victim. They were one and the same man, and ribboning himself with the instrument jerking like a composer's wand in his hand.

Mace and James turned to look at each other, as synchronous a response as their aspiration towards oblivion. But neither found the other looking back as the music of the mutilator suddenly withered down a long tunnel to the single concentrated note of a great chain giving under stress.

Confounded, fragmented, but nothing so much as consumed by the lust, the two halves of the one man who had hidden under the bridge descended on the whirlwind to have a bath in its ecstasies themselves.

I drove the Dodge pickup off the county highway and onto the abandoned logging road. As evergreen limbs slapped the windshield and overgrown bushes scraped the sides, I wondered if the truck would make it all the way through the wooded hills and, more importantly, if, in the dark of the midnight moon, we could find the old mine tunnel and Strickland's body again.

I glanced at Adrian. She was sitting in the passenger seat acting all Bette Davis cool while softly humming Jim Morrison tunes. *Acting.* The dashboard lights reflected the sweat christening her face.

My hand patted my shirt pocket searching for the Marlboro cigarettes that I had stopped smoking fifteen years ago. Adrian and I had committed the perfect murder and had gotten away with it . . . until the California Highway Commission announced the route of the new freeway.

"Val, this is it," Adrian said, pointing at a turnabout in the road. "This is the spot."

"You're wrong," I replied. "We're still too close to the highway. The mine is farther back. Near those two odd-shaped boulders."

Adrian nodded her head, remembering. "Oh, yeah. We called them the Lovers. Hey, do you think Strickland will be happy to have some visitors after all these years?"

I didn't answer.

We had killed Adrian's husband, who was a well-liked cop, but the case was listed as a Missing Persons because Strickland's cop pals had never found the body. Luck or fate or whatever you want to call it had been with us that day and the days following.

Adrian reported Strickland missing three days after we'd killed him. My idea. She acted all upset and teary-eyed during the interview with the police detectives. Her idea. The cops knew she was faking. Around the station house, everyone from the chief to the jailhouse janitor, knew that Adrian had been holding a mattress marathon with an Irish-Mexican kid named Valdez Ryan who was the assistant director at the local history museum. Everyone knew except for stupid, naïve Strickland.

The investigating detectives might have pressed more—they leaned hard on me—if they hadn't found Strickland's Ford Mustang dumped in the lake. My idea. They pulled the car out of the water and discovered plastic-wrapped LSD and reefer hidden under the wheel well. Adrian's idea. Immediately, the opinion that Strickland made the guys on the *Dragnet* TV show look like rogue vigilantes changed. He was dirty. The general consensus was that Strickland had crossed his underworld buddies and they had either turned him into trout bait or used him as part of a concrete foundation for a new building.

And we walked away clean.

I stopped the truck and cut the engine. Slowly, I slid out of the cab and studied the landscape. This looked like the right place but it looked wrong, too. As I boy, I had hiked all over these hills, knew them like I knew the lay of my own backyard, but I hadn't been here since the day we'd killed Strickland. How long had it been? LBJ was President then, US troop arrivals were increasing in Vietnam, the Beatles were still together, and we hadn't landed on the moon yet.

Adrian walked into the glare of the headlights and shined her flashlight into the trees. The years hadn't been kind to her. The slender, long-legged girl who had run naked with me through these very hills was gone. The woman in her place weighed two-and-a-half times what that girl did and wore orthopedic sneakers on varicose-veined legs that looked like Los Angeles road maps.

I had aged much better. Yes, I had. I weighed less than I did then thanks to my ulcer and my thick, dark hair had turned white and fallen out In clumps before I was thirty-five.

"Must be farther up the road," I said.

Adrian steadied her flashlight. "This is it."

I followed the line of her beam. The boulders that we had named the Lovers had toppled over and broken into rumble. Earthquake, maybe. Or, maybe, they had just collapsed because of stress and time.

"Let's get this done, Val," Adrian ordered.

That's what she had said then, too.

In my boyhood hikes through the hills, I had discovered an old mine that wasn't listed in the county or museum records. I figured, from the trash I found, that it had been dug in the early 1850s. The miners had tunneled straight into the hill about seventy-five yards then burrowed down at a steep angle several hundred more yards. If the mine had ever yielded any gold ore, there was no sign. My guess was that the miners had worked the place for about two years before giving up and no one had been inside until I came along.

I gathered the tools and burlap sack from the rear of the truck. With Adrian leading the way, we moved into the woods. Our plan was good. We'd gather up Strickland's bones and Monday, while I was working at the museum, I'd sneak down to the basement and dump him with the other bones stored there. No one would ever find him.

We killed Strickland because neither Adrian nor I could afford a divorce attorney. Simple economics and hell-for-leather lust had sealed his demise.

Adrian lured him to the wooded hills on the pretext of having a picnic. She insisted that he take along his birthday present—a double-barreled Remington twelve-gauge shotgun. She told him that he could do some target shooting. She told me that, if he suspected anything, she wanted him to have a false sense of security.

Shortly after they arrived, Adrian pretended to find the mine. She lit the lantern I'd left for her at the entrance then slipped inside. Strickland, carrying his shotgun, followed her.

I was already there, waiting.

I remember clearly aiming my .45 pistol at him and being unable to pull the trigger. Adrian didn't have my problem. She pulled her .22 revolver from her jacket pocket and shot him square in the back. Strickland spun around, stunned, confused. I swear he said 'ouch.' I fired a second later and the bullet slammed into his chest. He crashed into the mine wall and dropped into a sitting position. He stared at us, still uncomprehending, for a long moment then he thumbed the twin hammers of the shotgun back. Adrian shot him through the left eye.

We ducked outside and pulled loose the entry supports. Rocks and dirt collapsed downward, sealing Strickland's tomb.

Forever.

We thought.

In the dark, using a flashlight, stumbling more than once, it took us an hour to find the old mine. Grass and weeds had grown up through the dirt but I recognized the spot. I leaned against my shovel and gazed at the ground.

"What are you waiting for?" asked Adrian.

"Do you want me to do it?"

"I'll do it."

"Then let's get at it. The bugs are eating me alive."

I stabbed the shovel into the hillside and the topsoil collapsed, like water spinning down a drain, revealing the entrance. Adrian and I glanced at each other. The freeway construction crew would have definitely found this.

Dead air lingered heavy and stale in the entrance. My ulcer knife-twisted and I leaned against the shovel to keep from dropping onto all fours.

Adrian sighed. "When did your balls shrivel up into raisins, Val?" She shook her head. "I'm so glad I didn't stay with you."

Thank God for that! I wanted to yell. A week after we killed Strickland, Adrian left me for a real estate broker named Carver. Seems she'd been stepping out with him for months. Everyone knew. Everyone except stupid, naïve Valdez Ryan. Adrian married Carver and some time later the broker was murdered by a never-cap-tured burglar. I'd heard that Adrian later married a dance instructor then a tavern owner. Both those husbands died in freak accidents. Adrian had perfected her act and learned the proper way to collect on insurance policies.

Me, on the other hand, I'd spent the years going to work then straight home. I lost contact with all my old friends and didn't make any new ones. I hadn't gone out with a woman since Adrian. I just waited, waited for the cops to finally figure out what actually happened and come and collect me. I was still waiting.

Adrian flicked the flashlight on high beam, grabbed the burlap sack and ducked into the mine.

I inhaled deeply, watching stones continue to roll slowly down the hillside. I gripped the shovel—might need it if the opening caved-in—then stepped inside.

Immediately, a dark chill webbed down my spine. Adrian stood near Strickland haloing the young cop in her flashlight beam. He was still in the sitting position where he had fallen and died, still gripping his double-barreled shotgun. He was all dusty skeleton, flesh and meat long gone. Although now moldy tattered rags, I recognized the clothes he'd been wearing—turtleneck sweater, bell-bottomed pants, and high-top sneakers. Red Ball Keds to be exact. I bit into my lower lip. I was most certainly damned for this.

"Looks like he's smiling," Adrian said. "I think he *is* happy to see us."

Dirt sprinkled down from the ceiling.

"Quiet," I whispered, waving falling dust away from my face. "This whole thing could come down on us."

"Get your butt over here and put him in the bag," she snapped.

I couldn't move. It was as if I'd become rooted to the mine floor. I stared at Adrian then at Strickland's bones. I knew what I had to do. I'd spent ten thousand nights thinking about it.

"No," I said. The word sounded good, sounded so right. "I'm going to the cops. We have to atone for this."

Adrian turned toward me. She was holding a pistol—a .38 revolver this time—in her plump fist. "I thought you might turn completely worthless on me. Guess I'll just have to dump you and Strickland down the shaft and take my chances."

"Wait!" I started to shout.

Adrian fired. The bullet caught me below the navel. I clutched my gut, gasping, pressing my hands against the gaping wound, and folded onto my knees.

The gunshot echoed loudly. The old mine tunnel rumbled angrily in response and dirt vibrated from the ceiling and walls. Earth and stones tumbled into the entrance. As I curled onto my side, knowing I deserved this, I looked up at Adrian.

I saw it all.

Strickland's skull rolled off his body, his turtleneck-cloaked chest collapsed inward, and his skeletal finger tightened around the shotgun triggers. Both barrels of the Remington roared and shredded Adrian's head from her shoulders.

The skull lay facing me. It did look like he was smiling.

As I crawled toward the tunnel entrance, I knew that Adrian had been right. Strickland was happy to see us.

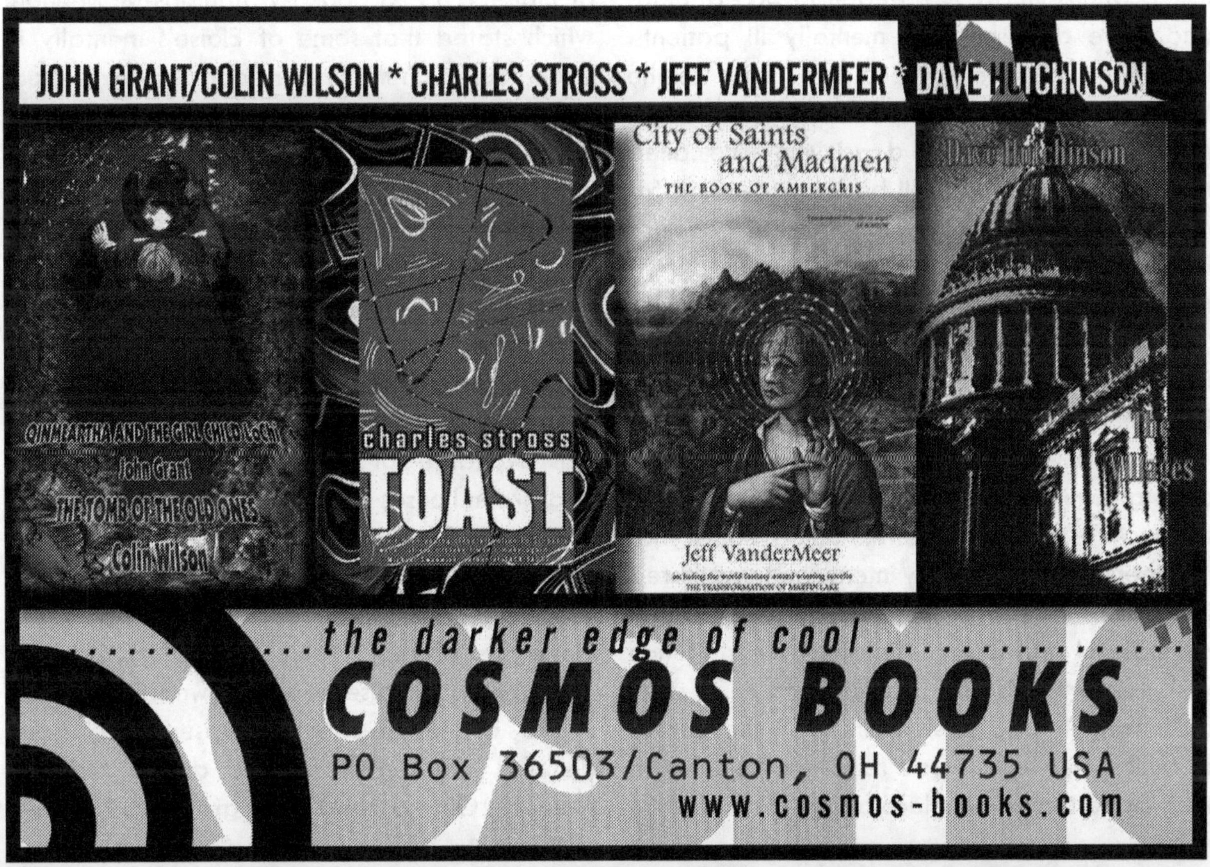

"ELOISE"

By Karen Carpenter

Imagine a place where babies, the poor and the blind reside alongside tuberculosis patients, alcoholics, thieves and the criminally insane. A hell-hole where innocent children lay awake nights, praying that the howling madman in the next bed won't chew through his leather arm restraints.

From 1839 until 1981, such a place did exist—in various stages and under numerous names. Mostly, the establishment was known as "Eloise", named in 1894 after a Detroit post-master's four-year-old daughter.

Actually, this institution first opened its doors in 1832, as a home for the poor. But after changing locations in 1839, it began to accept more and more diseased and mentally ill patients. Frequently the locals referred to Eloise as the "Crazy Hospital". And still today, many people swear that the anguished dead, who once called this asylum home, can still be heard wailing for mercy across the marshy wetlands that was once Eloise. Ghost hunters claim to have captured those spirits on film.

In a recent article for the *Detroit News*, Mary Bailey wrote: "For generations of metro-area Detroiters, Eloise Hospital stood at the corner of Michigan Avenue and Merriman Road as a chilling reminder of what could happen to you if your life took a bad turn." Bailey noted that nineteenth-century society intentionally gathered its feeble-minded, spastics, needy, diseased and mentally ill and tossed them into this institution with its drunkards and brawlers—to keep them all conveniently out of sight. In 1839, that corner of Michigan Avenue was a remote location. And thus, Eloise became a place of last resort for the downtrodden.

At one point in her later years, Eloise was recognized as one of the finest hospitals in the nation. But her early days were plagued by reports that patients were regularly beaten and subjected to overcrowding and unsanitary conditions. Doctors knew little about treating mental disease back then, and many subjected their patients to painful restraints and electric shock therapy. It's even been alleged that doctors at Eloise, handsomely rewarded by the pharmaceutical industry, used their patients as drug-testing guinea pigs.

In her article, Baily referenced *The History of Eloise*, a 1913 book by Stanislas M. Keenan, which stated that some of Eloise's mentally ill were housed on the upper floor of a farm structure, a building where pigs were kept. Keenan wrote that people in the vicinity heard "the chained unfortunates roaring and shrieking in discord with the squealing pigs beneath."

In her prime, the Eloise compound housed 10,000 "patients", in 75 buildings, on 902 acres. And she was entirely self-sufficient, boasting a keeper's residence, a library, bakery, cannery, fruit cellar and coffee shop. Affordable housing was available for the employees. Eloise even had green houses—and tobacco and dairy and pig farms. Eventually, Eloise became a city onto herself with her own power plants, sewage disposal, fire and police departments—even the Eloise post office.

Inevitably, Eloise had her own morgue, and 7,100 of her resident's corpses have been dumped into a Potter's field across Michigan Avenue. Only a handful of graves (593) have been marked, and those only with numbers. The Ford Motor Company, which purchased much of the land where Eloise once stood, recently began cleaning up the cemetery. And *The Friends of Eloise*, a current-day organization, is attempting to match the marked numbers of the dead with names in a register. But for over a half century, the burial grounds beyond the tall Pine trees, remained unkempt and unattended, as weeds grew over the morbid secrets of the dead.

Most of Eloise's buildings, with her clandestine patient files, have been razed. Only a few structures of the once massive compound remain. Today, a five-story brick building (The Kay Beard Building, built in 1931) houses the offices of a few social agencies and The Eloise Museum. One powerhouse, a bakery and commissary, and the old fire station still stand, though all are decaying. And one can still see the name ELOISE, painted in black letters across the smokestack of the old power plant.

Many curious people are drawn to the site. Some claim to have found torture devices and disturbing medical records scattered throughout Eloise's ruins and underground tunnels. One person discovered a cigarette lighter mounted on a cracked wall. The patients had inhaled nicotine to ease their suffering. The lighter still worked, glowing an eerie orange.

Messages on Eloise Internet sites convey the other-worldly sense of dread that visitors experience when they encounter the last vestiges of Eloise:

"You walk in there and you can just feel that they're all around."

"The company I work for was hired because of Satanic Activity in the power house."

"My daughter still talks about the Shadow People."

One of Eloise's callers, Mark Boone, wrote: "Those deemed insane have been traditionally locked away, experimented on and treated like lost souls often because they just chose not to play the world's game of rationalization."

Perhaps there is something to be learned from those restless spirits who still roam the marshy wetlands beyond Michigan Avenue. Or maybe we'd just like to convince ourselves that thousands of Eloise's nameless residents didn't suffer and die in vain. After all, mankind really does have an almost irresistible need to play the world's game of rationalization. We play, or else—we suffer the consequences.

"Listen. Don't put me on hold again. I'll just hang up. I've seen enough cop shows. Yes, Leah Patrick. No! All right, Ok, connect me. I won't hang up if you connect me.

"Detective . . . Yes, I do remember you. You were the bald man with glasses and white socks. I remember you very well. What? I'm sorry I had to leave. They were going to rape me. What? I could tell. Well if you have it on tape then you saw. You shouldn't have left me alone with them.

"Of course I won't tell you where I am. No, it's not a phone booth. No, there's no one here. No, I didn't hurt anyone. No. They were all dead when I got here. In a way I was glad. It's not easy being a girl. People are always trying to hurt you. And they're so much bigger and stronger.

"Sergeant Florrin? He was the fat guy? You shouldn't have left him alone with me. And that other one. No, I didn't rip his throat out. How could I do that? I'm only a girl. Well, yes. Right. That's right. I took both of their guns. For protection. One was all used up, I think. I threw it away before I left. Ok, then. So? You know, the police station isn't very safe. You shouldn't have left me alone with them. It wasn't right. Of course it's not safe! Just consider the fact that I could walk right out should tell you anyone could walk right in and do anything to a girl.

"These people here? The mother was shot. The children have their necks torn out. There are three of them. No, of course I don't know when it happened! They were dead when I got here.

"I don't know. It just looked like a good place. Yes, I told you before—it *was* convenient for me. I was very glad they were dead. Sometimes it works out that way. No. How can I be lucky when men are always attacking me? It's a good thing this woman here was dead, because she looks like she would have attacked me herself. There's something in her eyes. You never can know about people. There are lesbians, too—aren't there?

"Sergeant Florrin's wallet? Why would I take that? Three kids, too? So? I can't tell her hair color. There's nothing left but her eyes and all the blood . . . It's hard to imagine Sergeant Florrin having a wife and three kids and give me that look. But I got away. It wasn't easy.

"You? I think you mean well. You're just not very competent. Your captain? —how could it be your fault if I just walked out. I mean, you shouldn't have trusted those men with me—I do think that. He shouldn't blame you though if anybody could walk in or out of the police station.

"How should I know how many men were dead? All right. All right. I'll check. Let me look. Give me a second. Ok. There's no tops on any of the bullets, and they smell. Does that mean they've all been fired. Then this gun isn't any good to me? Thank you. I'll have to get another one. What are you saying? How would I know why all of the shells have been fired? It wasn't *my* gun!

"I think I'd better be going now. You say you want to help me, but then you left me alone with those men who tried to rape me. No . . . No . . . No. I don't think it does matter whether or not I'm attractive. It certainly doesn't seem to matter to men. If you do have it on tape then you know exactly what I mean!

"You want me . . . No. I can't. I won't. It's all right if her eyes are open. It's like, then, she's watching over her children. Mothers should do that. I know all about their having their own lives. I've certainly heard that enough. I know children are a burden, but they get born anyway. Yes, my mother? That's right—Vera. How did you know? My tattoos—by my tattoos . . . Of course. You're not stupid, just incompetent. I don't know how many. I never counted. All over-some you won't ever get to see. I don't know. I don't. I—oh, a hundred, give or take. That many, yes. Or more.

"You don't? She died in prison. Pneumonia. What? She tried to kill me. That's why I limp. I was in the hospital for three months. Yes, hip, knee—all of that. A chair. I don't know. I passed out. I woke up in the hospital. Well why do you think? —boys. I can't blame her, I guess. She just knew how they were. Oh, her boyfriend. Yes. Fourteen. I was fourteen. What? What do *you* have to be sorry about?

"Look, I have to go. I hear sirens. I have to go now. There must be a fire. A big one—lots of sirens. I can't tell from where. No, I don't know where. Listen, I can hardly hear you. I better go. I'll talk to your captain for you. What? He shouldn't blame you for me leaving—that's why. That's not right. It wasn't your fault the police station wasn't safe. I can't hear you! The sirens. I'll find out where he lives and talk to him. I'm sure I can make him understand."

Jack Fisher
What Lives Among the Skies

It left footprints in the snow on the roof.

They weren't actual human footprints because they weren't in the shape of a shoe or a boot, but they were three toe-like extensions pressed deep and firm into the snow.

Mr. Mort—a seventy year-old retired book-keeper and widow—had first come to realize something visited the skies at night when he heard a thunking somewhere up on his roof just weeks after his wife had died.

At first he thought it was a mother raccoon settling her babies in the attic or squirrels nesting in the vents . . . or perhaps his wife's ghost dancing up there. Being alone, he had often scared himself. The friggin' kids in the town made it no better for the poor old man. They egged his house, busted mailbox after mailbox until there was nothing but shards of plastic and twisted metal, and decorated his front yard with toilet paper every now and then.

Every week on his way to the grocery mart about eight blocks from his home, they would follow behind him in the shadows, the whole time whispering and laughing. "Looks like he shit his pants!" And then they'd get all serious. They would run up alongside of him and warn him of the night and what lived *in* it. He would never reply; he never even looked at the jerks, but his thoughts spun furiously.

"They know my wife is dead, so they like to scare me, an old man," he thought. *"It is they who I should fear. They rule the night . . ."*

Once the kids had sailed up on his roof and stuffed acorns and pine needles compacted with a snow laced with pebbles of ice down the chimney. In his boxer shorts, he had to go up there in that hungry wind and dislodge the smoking mess, trembling in fear of what might grab him from the eaves.

Exhausted, he pressed his back to the ancient brick chimney and slid down it where he sat comfortably in mother nature's white padding-praying that he wouldn't have to call out to anyone in the town for help from atop his own roof—and watched the magnificent storm clouds of smoke billow from the choked chimney. The wind flipped his hair and his T-shirt flapped against his bony chest, making sounds like flags in the wind.

Mr. Mort was just about to get up (after the December winds finally offered him back his breath) when he heard something amongst the treetops.

A fast rustling.

It was like someone had thrown a corpse through their tops.

Mr. Mort stood and the gust picked up again. There it was. He could see a cloud of blackness, growling like mountain cats and cart wheeling his way. It roiled forth with storm-like velocity and went over the rooftop with shredded tendrils of what seemed to be a black material spinning wildly from an indecipherable frame. It sailed its shadow across December roofs and as it passed, it looked down at him and smiled, its eyes concealed in darkness.

He balled himself against the chimney, his eyes on the beast until it landed about thirteen rooftops away from his. He watched—the whole time shaking with lines of saliva running from his mouth and being taken away by the wind—as it spun like a whirlwind of crows before it actually stood like a human on the peak of one of the houses and threw its black arms up to the sky, silhouetted against a perfectly round, full moon.

. . . and then he remembered beginning to shake so terribly that he had to lay his head down against the icy snow where he fell asleep. And there he slept.

He woke up to a sky that threatened snow in the early hours of the morning.

The creature was gone.

Before dusk the next evening, Mr. Mort attempted sitting out on the front porch in hopes of catching the little bastards that had clogged his chimney the night before with last night's encounter fresh on his mind, but he never caught them. He saw not a soul out on the streets.

In a town where children whispered secrets in the classroom about being monsters and wrote about them on walls and on the sidewalks were— surprisingly—empty, except for the paper mice that blew up Into the trees and down the gutters and the stray sheets of newspaper—probably decades old!—sliding everywhere and, of course, the writing on the sidewalks that read: *"Mr. Mort is an old bastard"* or *"An old shit lives here"* with an arrow pointing to the steps of his porch or: *"What lives at night can kill"* written in sidewalk chalk or with broken white stones.

Surely they knew what flies across the rooftops at night, he thought.

The sun finally set in the horizon and he gave the deserted down one last glaze before bed and then headed in.

The house was dark. He'd forgotten to turn on the lights. He had no idea he'd be staying out front so late. Seconds after Mr. Mort closed the front door—even it just was the front door—he heard a giggle from above.

In the attic . . .

"Mae? Is that you?" he asked, talking to the ceiling. "Don't you be scarin' me . . ."

Nothing.

"Ridiculous . . ." he mumbled and walked into the kitchen where he cracked open a beer on the countertop and sat in his tired recliner in front of the TV. Soon, though, he remembered that he shouldn't get too comfortable. It was too quiet out; it was nighttime and trouble lurked among shadows when the sky was as black as coal. He knew it. God forbid he let himself fall asleep.

There was another noise upstairs in the attic. Like something heavy being pulled across the floor; something dead. Mr. Mort got up, straightened himself out, and gathered enough courage to venture up the stairs.

He walked slowly, looking at the brown, curling wallpaper in dismay, and then to his faded loafers. He had a question for his shoes that sat on the tip of his tongue: "Do you think I should go up there?" but they didn't reply.

Sssssssssh-thunk. Sssssssh-thunk.

The hackles on the back of his neck and along the tops of his arms were tickled and they stood all-erect and shivering, like a grasshopper's legs frictioned together. The stairway became darker as he ascended. His mind was a wonderful conglomerate of fear. He feared this—huddled children hiding in the shadows all innocent except for mouth's full of razors, or his wife's voice whispering too close to his ear, or what he'd do if he stumbled over a body.

It was completely dark and he blinked his eyes to make sure that they were really still open. His feet moved slowly. He felt his way through the dark and made his way to the middle of the hallway. There was scarce light being thrown from the plug-in night-light in his bathroom down at the end of the hall and it was just enough so that he was able to locate the pull string to the attic stairs.

He faltered at first, regained his balance and then groped for the string again. With shaking hands, he pulled the attic stairs down and unfolded them onto the floor, gave them one good push to lock them in place (and to see if they don't break into dust motes), and began to climb them, slightly hesitant at first, and then confident again that it was nothing.

Jesus . . . what am I doing, he thought.

The noise was gone and had been for about eight minutes. He almost started to climb back down the stairs when soon enough he heard it again, only this time it was closer . . . maybe a few feet into the darkness.

. . . and then it stopped.

He had already climbed the stairs and was standing among dust. It was very hot and musty considering that it was about thirty degrees out. His knees finally buckled with terrible fear and he crawled, dying to lean his aching and frightened back against an encrusted wall for a minute, to wait for his heart to stop pounding and his hands to stop shaking. He had already forgotten that something was up there with him.

"I'm too old for this, goddammit," he heaved, closing his eyes to the blackness that already was.

Leaning against a wall with what felt like exposed beams, he continued to try and calm himself. He took in deep breathes through his nose and released them from out his mouth. The attic felt alive and sounded like it was breathing. The beams were damp and moist and the air was thick and muggy. For support, Mr. Mort used the wall he was leaning on to get up. His fingers pressed into something warm like a mouth—it was wet, slippery, and he felt the fleshy mass of a tongue.

He hoisted himself up onto his feet, his heart beating until his chest ached.

A heart attack . . .

There was a thin ray of light coming up from the hallway (the bathroom night-light) and that was his target. Behind him, there was scrambling like someone or something getting up onto its feet and then thunking. Something was moving and it was behind him. Running. Claws tapped the floorboards.

His brow furrowed. "My God!" And began to bend as he approached the stairs, ready to climb down them as fast as his old legs would allow him. Whatever was coming came quickly. The nails on the hard wood became louder. Mr. Mort's hands shook and he began to cry.

As he hurried down the stairs backwards he stuttered, "Mae? Is that you, Mae?"

It wasn't.

He looked up before he stepped onto the last step and silhouetted against the shadows was something horribly inhuman. Something with thorny knees, thick claws, and webbed appendages.

The mocking voices of the children sang to him: "Old Mr. Mort, the crazy old bastard" like a mantra. And then he began to sing the words out loud like rhyming verse only scared little children would sing about what lurked in the shadows at night down by the sewers or what lives behind bathroom mirror's.

What lives at night can kill . . .

With tears running down his face and crying for his wife, Mr. Mort attempted to push the attic stairs back up, but the form—writhing in the darkness—wouldn't allow it. It bent down and shoved them back with hands that dripped Ichor from pores on its leathery skin that gasped and opened like tiny mouths.

Mr. Mort crab-walked backwards to the bathroom door and pushed it open wide with his back, salty piss warming his boxer shorts. The stairs were neither touching the floor nor totally closed, but hanging suspended in mid-air until they were kicked to the ground. The two bottom steps splintered and dust was summoned from the floorboards.

In the bathroom light, Mr. Mort—whose heart was slowly being seized—watched the beast come forth with a gaunt frame, clothed in shreds of blackness like that of an ancient street peasant with a mane of splinters and three claws that grew yellow and thick like tree bark from deep within its body. And as it came closer, closer into the better of the light, he noticed that its eyes were not in comparison with its hideous body. They were sky-blue and glassy; it had the eyes of a mischievous child, of something that ate cotton candy and giggled a lot.

Disturbing eyes, but not evil.

Wafts of delicious winds swirled around the hallway. It smelled neither of rot nor of piss or even the dank smells of Hell, but of dying ghosts and memories, of bubble gum and confection.

Almost-cute giggles echoed from the recesses of the attic—reverberated from the beast's skin—and bounced off the cobwebs in the corners of the hall. The inhuman being stood there, breathing heavily. Its chest cavity flexed in and out and its throat muscles looked like a thousand earthworms swallowing and digesting rot.

Voices came from the demon yet it's mouth did not move.

"*Mr. Mort, the night is alive and it is danger-ous . . . you stupid old bastard.*"

"Fucking . . . kids . . ." Mort whispered. He grasped the throat of his T-shirt and split it open, holding the area under which his heart beat a slow red.

And then he smiled with rivulets of tears reflecting the abomination before him—the source of his mockery, his demise. Everything became quiet and then bathroom light began to fade.

The beast bent down, its claws flexing, the mouths on its body chirping. With one last heavy breath, Mr. Mort took in a gasp of air, held it in and stared back at himself from the creatures' watery eyes . . . and then exhaled. His chest felt no better, only worse.

Fire licked up from behind its baby blue's before a silver film encased them for protection before the attack.

A thousand giggles echoed throughout the house, along the beautifully empty roads, and from among the skies . . .

. . . And then a black, swirling figure busted through the chimney and took flight, pin wheeling across the bold and happy moon. It launched itself with sinuous hind legs off of every other rooftop, it's belly warm with old blood.

The children of the town gathered and watched what it was that ruled the night sky, smiling with water-jewel eyes.

And then they tore off their faces.

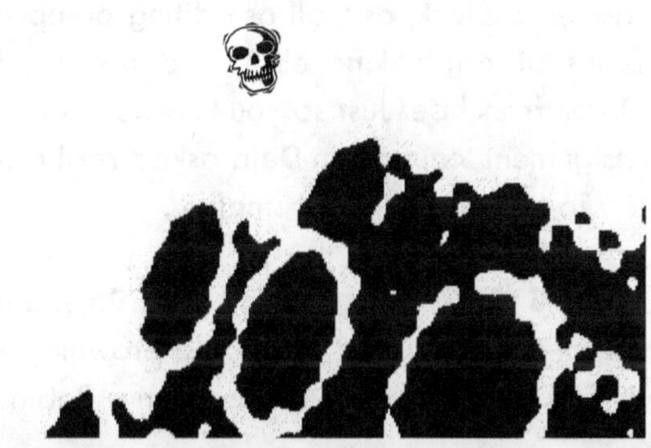

GRAPHIC VIOLENCE

steve roman

Welcome to the first installment of "Graphic Violence." This is the place that covers the comics beat. Sometimes there'll be more horror titles covered, sometimes more crime (though there are far more of the former out there to review than the latter). It's also the place that'll show there's more to horror and crime than just the works of The Two Brians: Michael Bendis and Azzarello. (Somebody's writing the other three comics out there, after all.)

Now, you're probably wondering what gives me the right to write on this subject. Here's the pedigree: I'm the writer/creator of *Lorelei*, a horror series I self-published between 1993 and 1995 (and which is currently being restarted), and for the book publishing house ibooks, inc., I'm overseeing the reissues of mysteries by authors like Loren D. Estleman, Cornell Woolrich, and Lawrence Block, as well as editing an upcoming series of original novels based on the *Law & Order* franchise. Just so you know. And I got the assignment 'cause Tom Deja asked real nice.

To begin, we'll start small.

CREEPS #1-2: Image Comics, $2.95/per issue.
Imagine what it'd be like if Tod Browning's classic film *Freaks* had been based on a Robin Cook medical thriller, and you've got a fair idea of this series from writer Dan Mishkin and artist Tom Mandrake. Set in an unnamed American city, the eponymous characters are the kind of homeless people you'd generally expect to find in Bernie Wrightson's darkest nightmares—grotesque, hideously misshapen, oozing bodily fluids and gases worse than any feeding frenzy at a bean-eating contest. Led by the robed and goateed Eyeball (who, of course, is blind), the *Creeps* are looking to punish the owners of a biotech company called Genesys for kidnapping some of their friends.

Why was this done? Well, there are no answers to be found in #1, which comes across as a standard, though confusing, introduction to the characters—confusing because there are just too many of them crammed in, with a promise of more to come as the story progresses. Unfortunately, Mishkin's superhero background comes to the fore here, with each character introducing his- or herself, or being introduced, as they make their entrance, and most of them have superheroish names (Breaker, Gelulite, Booger). And when we do get answers in #2, you can see the motives for Genesys' nebulously nefarious actions coming a mile away: genetic experimentation, and organ harvesting. On the other hand, Mandrake is in fine form, showing how grotesquely detailed he can get when set loose on a project that seems to fire his imagination.

VAMPIRELLA #4: Harris Comics, $2.95. There was a time when Vampirella was a pretty straightforward character. A refugee from a dying planet of not-undead vampires called Darkulon, she came to Earth in search of blood, only to find out our world was filled with more people interested in sacrificing her to some Elder Gods than in bedding a woman with supermodel looks and a fashion sense that didn't go beyond a couple of strategically-placed bits of cloth and a pair of go-go boots. (What's their problem?) But then, years later, Harris Comics got ahold of her and, with typical modern-day publishing thinking, immediately changed her origin—and her attitude—two or three times. It didn't make the new incarnations of Vampi any better—just different.

This is the first third of the "Fear of Mirrors" story arc written by John Smith, with art by Mike Mayhew. Smith is one of the folks who came over during the British Invasion that didn't catch fame and fortune, while Mayhew made his debut in Topps Comics' *Zorro* series, where he helped introduce the world to another bad girl: Lady Rawhide. It starts with a mysterious circus train materializing from a portal outside the town of Coogan's Bluff, New York (Clint Eastwood fans take note), then moves on to Vampi taking out a group of vampiric drug dealers in order to track down their leader. After eliminating him, a possessed victim of the vamps sudenly sits up and tells Vampi to head for New York to find "the black mirror" (Huh?) because "there are worse things out there than vampires."

Unfortunately, there's not much to recommend here. Smith's story does nothing but estab-

lish Vampirella as a true bad-ass, a task already handled by previous writer Mark Millar in his story arc, and Mayhew's art is so reference-heavy Harris could have cut out the middleman and just run the copious amounts of photographs the artist took for lightboxing purposes. Perhaps, as with *Creeps*, the story will pick up as it progresses. I can only hope the same can be said for the art.

So, that wasn't so bad a beginning, right? A bit brutal, but what's crime and horror without brutality? Next time around, we'll take a look at some of the European graphic novels Dark Horse Comics has begun releasing. Until then, as a great man once said, "Let's be careful out there." You never know who—or what—is lurking in the shadows.

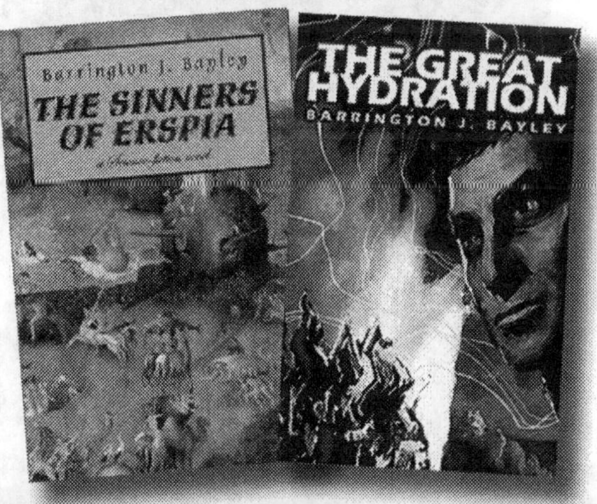

"THE MOST ORIGINAL SF WRITER OF HIS GENERATION"—MIKE MOORCOCK

chaos theory jason brannon

Framing each of his classmates in the scope of a high-caliber rifle, Foster searched for a glimpse of the kind of person he could have become. He wasn't disappointed that his life had veered away from the rest of these losers. He was simply thankful that he hadn't made those small, seemingly inconsequential choices that might have landed him in a similar shape. Of course, he knew a little more about the random mechanics of the world than any of these people did. He had read the journals explaining the idea of chaos science and subscribed to the hypothesis like a zealot in the grip of biblical prophecy.   According to theorists, events of monumental catastrophe could stem from the smallest of occurrences.   The fact that he had decided to attend the class reunion armed with an assault rifle was proof enough of that.

"Does the flapping of a butterfly's wings in Brazil set off a tornado in Texas?" he asked himself, imagining the mess he could make by simply squeezing the trigger. A butterfly in Rio flaps its wings, stirring up small eddies of air that create even greater pockets of atmospheric change. The effects reverberate around the world resulting in a Texas tornado. Yet, no one would ever suspect that the reason for shattered homes and broken bodies could stem from something so seemingly inconsequential as a flying Monarch. Still, Foster saw how powerful random occurrence could be everytime he looked in the mirror and saw his black mother and white father in the mix of his skin. Chance was the only thing that had lured his mother down that particular shadow-filled street. Chance was the only thing that had caused Foster's father to glance out of the window of his car at that moment in time. Of course, it was a little more than chance that drove that white man to pin that poor black woman down in the alley and take from her what he wanted. Still, Foster owed his entire life to chaos, chance, and a simple peek out the dirty window of an El Dorado. He had learned not to turn his back on who he was.

Remembering the way certain girls had laughed at him so many years before, Foster thumbed the safety off of his rifle when Cheri Arnold, class president, sauntered into the crosshairs. She still wore the same atrocious horn-rimmed glasses, but something about her had changed. No longer was she the shapeless wallflower. She had a woman's figure and a nice smile. Nonetheless, Foster's rifle was a time machine, and he knew with one tug on the trigger that he could transform Miss Cheri Arnold back into the hideous, misshapen thing she'd been in high school, only worse. From gorgeous to gore, she would be little more than a splatter on the dance floor, trodden underfoot by her classmates.

He nearly took the shot, but then decided that he didn't want to rush things. He had been waiting for this day for twenty years. A few more minutes wouldn't hurt.

He had arrived much earlier than everyone else and scurried up into the rafters, settling himself behind the scoreboard that was used during the basketball games. It was a perfect hiding place and a painful reminder of how isolated his teenage years actually were. He'd lived through the worst of it, however, and had returned to make sure that some of these people wouldn't. He only wondered how his former classmates would react when they realized that they were just as red on the inside as he was.

Foster remained perched behind the scoreboard for the next hour like a sentinel vulture, waiting on the fresh supply of carrion. He watched couples dance using the old steps they remembered from Prom Night, nerds comment on the teachers that were really tough, and bullies dart nervously in and out of the crowd hoping that nobody remembered them or the things they had done. Out of the cliques of people that were still intact, Foster seriously doubted that the bullies knew just how much power they'd been holding in their hands during those fateful years. All it took for them to loose the reins of chaos was one venomous slur, one practical joke, one backstabbing comment to start the horses of Armageddon galloping.

Thinking back on all he'd had to suffer through, it would have been so easy to end a few lives right then and there. Foster even thought with some humor that he could even keep a tally of the number he took out. After all, he was sitting on top of the scoreboard. But then he saw something that made him reconsider. That something was Jonas Ray.

The best Foster could tell the guy still seemed to need a course in personal hygiene. His hair was greasy and hung in long dark strands about his face. Sighting him through the rifle scope, Foster also saw that the teeth that weren't missing had bits of tobacco stuck to them like plankton on the hull of a sunken ship. Yet what he lacked in cleanliness, he strove to make up for in fashion. The tie he wore was absurdly wide, looking more like a dinner napkin than any fashion accessory. The coat was a hideous brown plaid that resembled the furniture upholstery on a couch that Foster had owned a long time ago. And the pants were flared at the bottom. Of course, it was all a man like Jonas Ray could afford, and he should have been respected for the modicum of effort. But that wasn't the way things went at Donnersville High School. That wasn't the way things worked in the world. The moment he stepped foot in the gym old girlfriends whispered behind their program of events and the old jocks elbowed each other in the ribs.

Out of all the people that had shown up for the reunion, Jonas Ray was the one person that Foster didn't intend to kill. As far as Donnersville High was concerned they were both pariahs.

As it turned out, Jonas Ray didn't want a brother in arms. He had all the friend he needed in his jacket pocket. Before Foster could put a new target in his sights, Jonas had the old handgun out and had covered the gymnasium floor in a slick red puddle. Foster almost reneged on his

vow to shoot Jonas right then and there, jealous that the man had stolen his moment of glory. But then he thought about the sorts of things that had been done to Jonas during his freshman year, and it wasn't so hard to understand why he had waltzed in ready to kill.

The football players had called Foster names. Those same athletes took a nude Polaroid of Jonas Ray while he was showering during phys ed class and posted it in the girl's locker room. The practical jokers had spiked Foster's soda in the cafeteria while he wasn't looking. They had filled Jonas Ray's with a liquid laxative, causing him to soil his pants in Mrs. Cole's geometry class. For every cruel punishment he had received at the hands of his classmates, Foster could remember at least one more terrible incident that had befallen Jonas. So while Foster was justified in his choice of a hunting rifle, Jonas Ray was severely underarmed for revenge. As much as he'd endured through life, he needed a neutron bomb to more adequately level the playing field.

Still, he seemed to be doing all right with his pistol.

Foster knew that he should have been happy to see his tormentors go down in a hail of bullets and gunsmoke, but something happened amidst the chaos that surprised him. For years, he had envisioned the day when he would brace the rifle against his shoulder, sight his target, and blow the top of some poor fool's head off for what they had done or said to him so many eons before. There were times when the scene was so real that he could actually see the chunks of skull splattering against the wall. And yet the real thing made him sick to witness. There was so much blood, so much mess.

Because everyone was running for cover, nobody saw the stream of vomit that splashed over the side of the scoreboard. Feeling suddenly like a coward, Foster tried to get hold of himself only to go into a series of dry heaves and retching. At best count, there were twelve people down, bleeding from numerous holes, staring sightlessly up at him as if he were some sort of avenging angel. And true enough, he had come here to kill. Only things were different now that Foster's grudge was finally put into perspective.

Having read every scientific journal he could get his hands that subscribed to the notion of chaos theory, Foster had never heard anyone suggest exterminating butterflies as a way to end storms. But the idea had some merit. Especially now that he could look back on what happened to him in high school and see how insignificant so much of it was.

Knowing that this would be the first and last time he would ever do such a grisly thing, Foster trained his rifle on the back of Jonas Ray's head and pulled the trigger. The man went down with his victims, and the outward moving ripples on the surface of the tempestuous pool of chaos gradually smoothed out and disappeared.

Still surprised by what he had done, Foster climbed down from the scoreboard. Once the roar of gunfire had quieted, some of those who had taken cover gradually stood up to survey the damage. Some of his classmates stayed where they were, sobbing quietly. Others were too shocked to make any sound. And still a few, like Cheri Arnold, saw what happened to Jonas Ray and recognized the man who had taken him out.

"Foster Duncan," she said, her hands trembling as though afflicted with a palsy. "That is you, isn't it?"

Foster nodded his head slowly.

"You saved lives today," she said. "You're a hero."

Foster sat down on the bleachers when there was no more feeling in his legs. He had never been anyone's hero, and he needed time to let what Cheri had said sink in. He had saved the very people he had come here to kill, and he wasn't at all sure why he'd done it. In the distance he could hear sirens as the police and ambulances sped to the scene. Closer, he could hear the heavy plod of more footsteps coming toward him.

"Duncan, you're a good man. That was some quick thinking on your part. None of the other hunters in the group thought to run to their vehicles and arm themselves. You did, and most of us are alive because of it."

Foster looked up and was surprised to see McGraw Johnson, Jonas Ray's photographer and administrator of liquid laxatives. Never in a million years would he have expected to hear any kind words toward him come from that mouth, and yet, Johnson had all but given him a thank-you kiss on the lips.

Foster still couldn't bring himself to like McGraw Johnson. In fact, after all he'd seen and felt, Foster still wanted Johnson dead. But not like this. Not in a hail of bullets and a spattering of blood. Understandably, after all his plotting and dreams of blood, it was somewhat of a relief to put his revenge on hold.

"Long time, no see," Foster said, extending his hand, briefly remembering the vicious rumors McGraw had started about his masculinity. Johnson shook it willingly, unaware of how close he was to nudging the bloom where a delicate butterfly waited.

Foster was glad that the butterfly which fueled his anger had taken time to find a flower and light, resting its influential wings for a spell. No tornado in the world would ever start without that priming breeze, and he had to admit that it felt good to bask in the sunshine for a while instead of pursuing the storms.

"Yeah, you did real good," McGraw said, slapping Foster on the back. "And I have to admit it surprised me a little. I would have never expected that of a half-breed."

Foster gritted his teeth and closed his eyes. All he could hear was the tiny patter of wings on the wind and the rumbling of cataclysm.

Doug Hewitt

The hostage situation wasn't all that different from others I'd witnessed—with one major exception. My wife was inside.

Lieutenant Hardaway nudged me and whispered, "Melon head's here."

The lieutenant and I were standing beside a fold-out card table on which sat clipboards, tape-recorders, and a telephone that was connected to the recorder. I turned and saw Joe Melton pedaling his one-speed bicycle amid the fire trucks, EMS vehicles, and squad cars, making his way across the parking lot. The emergency lights gleamed on his shiny bald head, giving him a macabre fun-house appearance.

"His name's Melton," I said. "Don't make that mistake again."

The lieutenant winced. "Sorry, Detective Krantz. Didn't mean anything by it."

Melton never complained about the nickname, but I knew he harbored a constant hurt inside. According to Melton, so did I—we share a need to find ways to live in a world that was falling apart around us.

In the five years since I met him at a stress reduction seminar, Melton had helped me—and no one else on the police force—with small disturbances. Domestic disputes. An occasional suspect holed up. But never when a crowd was nearby.

I pushed the lieutenant aside, ducked yellow crime-scene tape, and hurried through the crowd.

Melton would need my help. He couldn't handle crowds. He hated them. He tended to lose his breath and pass out.

Most of the people in the crowd were emergency personnel, but there were reporters and next-of-kin, too. Newscasters stood in front of cameras and spoke overly loud, giving the particulars of the case.

Rappahannock College . . .

Fredericksburg, Virginia . . .

Twenty-eight hostages inside . . .

One confirmed death . . .

I reached Melton, who stood at the edge of the crowd. He dropped his bicycle to its side. "Hello, Krantz," he said, his accent thickly British.

"Thanks for coming."

I gently held Melton's arm and led him toward the building's side entrance. Maybe physical contact would keep Melton's attention away from the swarm of emotions that were bombarding his uniquely receptive mind.

"Nasty business, this," Melton said.

"I'm going crazy worrying about Gloria."

"You two have a special connection. It transcends this world, you know."

"Let's just keep that connection intact, okay?"

"Is she all right?"

"As far as I know," I said. "But one of the kids is dead. Murdered. The sonofabitch killed her to show us he means business. His name's Baine.

He's holding Gloria and twenty-seven students hostage. Room one-eighteen."

"I must talk to him," Melton said, slowly shaking his large head, which appeared more bulbous than it actually was because he kept it shaved. "When I do, you wait outside the classroom."

If Melton held to form, my job would be easy.

"It's good you didn't quit the force like you threatened," Melton said. "No one else would've called me."

"Don't worry about them. They just don't understand you."

"They laugh at my melon head."

"They act like immature kids sometimes."

"But you and I are mature, right? We understand life and death. We don't laugh much."

I hesitated. "Not much."

"Which is why you wanted to retire."

"But I didn't, so I was here to call you, to ask for your help. That's good, right?"

"I believe I can help."

"I hate to put you in danger."

"It's not the danger I'm afraid of," Melton said, eyeing the crowd.

I led him by reporters jabbering into hand-held mikes. Couples that I assumed were parents of the kids inside hugged each other and cried. Melton stumbled twice, but we made it through the crowd. As we neared the side of the building, Lieutenant Hardaway called me —"Lieutenant Krantz!" he said, waving the telephone. "Baine wants to talk to you."

"Come on," I said, pulling Melton.

At the table, the lieutenant handed me the phone. I held my hand over the mouthpiece and asked, "Did you tell him we have a negotiator coming?"

"He didn't give me a chance," Lieutenant Hardaway said. "He demanded to talk to you.

Just you."

"Any idea why?"

"I think he trusts you."

I had spoken to Baine briefly, making sure that the situation inside was stable. I had stalled, not wanting anyone to do anything until Melton arrived. Besides, the captain had turned the situation over to the SBI, so I had no authority. The captain was a gun-shy, by-the-book college boy, hesitant to take charge of a situation. He had called in a SWAT team from Norfolk.

I raised the handset to my mouth. "Krantz here."

"I'm ready to make my demands," Baine said. His voice was calm, matter-of-fact, and throaty. I imagined he was a large man.

"A release of hostages is customary at this point," I said. "It'll show us you're dealing in good faith."

"You'll just have to trust me, Krantz. Tell you what, I won't kill anyone for now."

"What do you mean, for now?"

"That depends on you."

"I see. Tell me your demands. I promise to do my best."

"First, I want you to know something. I hate that I'm forced to go this far. I only want what's best for the country. Hell, I have it all worked out. It's a great plan, but what good is it if no one hears it? Nobody listens to people like me. They'll listen now, and that's all I ever wanted."

"Tell me your plan," I said.

"I want the right people here so they can listen to my demands. A senator, a congressman, and a judge. Three branches of government. This way, it'll be binding. And I want three people from the media. A TV anchor, a radio newscaster, and a newspaper reporter."

"It'll take time to get those people together."

"I want to be reasonable, but I'm warning you—I hate getting jerked around."

"If these people come and listen, you'll release the hostages?"

"Only if they enact my plan. And if you try to trick me, if I think someone is pretending to be someone, I'll kill another hostage."

"We'll meet your demands. Just don't panic."

"I'm extremely calm. Rational. I've thought this through, see? By the way, if I see any attempt at a rescue, a hostage dies. Or maybe I'll kill all of them. We can negotiate something like that."

"I have to check something. I'll get back to you soon." I handed the receiver to the lieutenant and stepped back.

It was just past noon. The temperature was getting hot.

"Call the captain," I told the lieutenant. "Make sure he knows what Baine wants."

"The captain'll be here in a few minutes."

"What about the SBI?"

"On the way. No ETA yet."

"If Baine calls again, stall."

I took Melton's arm and led him along the crime-scene tape to the side of the building. A sergeant stood there, arms folded across his chest. "Detective Krantz? What are you doing here?"

"The captain wants me inside," I said.

"I was told to keep everyone out. If the captain wants you inside, he has to tell me."

"I'm not fucking around. My wife's in there."

"I have my orders."

Melton touched the sergeant's arm. "Don't take things so seriously. Relax. See the leaves? They're beautiful, right? Warm, fall colors. Burgundy and gold. Quite calming."

Waves of serenity radiated from Melton's head like ripples of warm wind. Soft melodies of wind. Warm breezes. Very calming. Swinging the mood of the sergeant. Sedating him.

Seeing the sergeant's eyes glaze, I pulled Melton under the tape. We continued into the building.

I stopped just inside the door, reached under my jacket, and pulled out a handgun from one of my shoulder harnesses. Noticing a flurry of movement, I peered back through the door window. The SBI caravan had arrived. Teams surged forward with riot shields, pushing onlookers aside.

"The captain will be glad they're here," I whispered. "If the SBI screws up, he blames them. If they succeed, he takes the credit."

"Ah, a hidden agenda," Melton said.

"And the captain will say he had no choice. He had to call in the SBI because Baine is killing people."

"He's not killing now," Melton said.

"How do you know?"

Melton frowned, shifted his weight, scratched his arm.

"Through your psychic abilities?" I asked.

"Yes. Were you wanting me to explain them? You asked how I knew."

"I just want to know if you're certain. I want to know if that bastard has a gun aimed at my wife."

"I sense no terror."

"So you don't think he'll shoot anyone soon?"

"I can't predict. You know that. Don't ask the impossible."

"Okay, okay. "I hesitated. "Do you feel a connection with Baine?"

"I sense him, his mood. He's calm, but impatience niggles at him."

"Can you make a connection with the captain?" I asked. "I want to know if he'll hold back the SBI while we're inside."

Melton closed his eyes. A few seconds later, he shuddered. "He is a cold man."

"And?"

"He knows we're in. He wants to wait and see what happens to us."

"You're sure?"

"The captain is easier to read than Baine. Baine's difficult. I'll have to get close to him."

"How close?"

"Arm's reach."

"That's too close."

"Everything works out for the best."

"Sometimes I think you could use a good dose of uneasiness."

"And you need to learn to calm yourself. Peace of mind has to be learned."

"Maybe you could make me calm."

"If people want true peace of mind, they have to rely on themselves."

I grunted. "I'll work on it first thing after we get Gloria out of there." I turned toward the main hallway and spotted a wall-mounted phone with its receiver off the hook, perhaps the one Baine had called from. "Is Baine in the classroom?"

"Yes."

I stepped slowly ahead, keeping near the wall, edging past school offices. After turning into the main hallway, I heard Baine's voice projecting from a bullhorn, probably out the classroom window: "Listen to me, everyone. How many of you have complained about the government? Be honest. You are Americans. Unite now. Force the police into doing things my way. They're not cooperating."

I edged past room one-fourteen.

Baine continued: "The next death will be on your hands. It'll be your fault if you don't insist the authorities meet my demands."

"He sees what he's doing as rational," Melton whispered. "He sees himself as a hero. But there are undercurrents of despair."

"What do you mean?" I asked.

"He was recently divorced."

Baine's voice strengthened, as though he had discovered the bullhorn's volume switch. "For

now, I just want to talk to a few people. What harm is there in that? Is it worth risking lives?"

"She left him suddenly, I think," Melton said.

We passed room one-sixteen.

Melton moaned. "I hate this."

"Are you okay?" Melton sometimes absorbed the emotions of the people he was trying to calm. On several occasions, I had almost called paramedics. But Melton had recovered quickly. There was no permanent damage, Melton claimed.

"Just keep going," Melton said.

We continued to the next classroom. Room one-eighteen. Baine had stopped talking. The quiet was unsettling. I could almost hear sweat running from my pores.

I looked back at Melton. "Ready?"

He nodded, his smile grim. "Wait here."

He moved by me and slowly entered the classroom.

I half-expected a gunshot.

But I heard nothing but silence.

As slowly as I could, I counted silently to ten.

Then, gripping my handgun, I peered around the doorframe.

Baine and Melton appeared to be in a stare-down, a contest to see who would blink first. Baine stood at the far end of the room, near the chalkboard. He held a bullhorn and wore a red motorcycle helmet. A gas mask hung from a shoulder strap. His flannel shirt revealed the outline of a Kevlar vest underneath. A duffel bag lay near his feet, along with scattered grenades, rifles, clips, and boxes of ammunition.

Chairs had been arranged in a circle in the middle of the room. A holding pen. The hostages, including Gloria, sat within. Their eyes were haunted. They shifted nervously like cattle smelling blood in a slaughterhouse.

The white-painted wall below the window was speckled red, and in the corner there was an axe, its blade stained with blood.

"Why are you so angry?" Melton asked softly, continuing to stare at Baine.

"How can you be so fucking calm?"

Melton took one step forward.

Baine blinked. His eyes danced with panic as he dropped the bullhorn. He picked up a rifle, grabbed a clip, and slapped it in.

Melton took another step.

"Stay back," Baine warned, his eyes widening.

"I only want to talk," Melton said, hands extended, palms up. "We're not so different, you and I. We want the same things."

"You some kind of shrink?"

"No, but you want peace of mind. I can feel it. I want the same thing."

"Yeah, it's what everybody wants. Except I'm doing something about it."

"A one-man revolution."

"Call it what you want."

I wiped sweat from my handgun's grip. I didn't have a clean shot at Baine, but maybe Melton would move. Or maybe Baine would step out of Melton's way. Maybe, maybe, maybe. I felt like a bomb with a timer set to trigger at random.

"I want to help," Melton said, taking another step.

Gloria's head angled toward the classroom door. Her eyes gleamed with recognition. "Jack!" she said softly, not overly loud, but loud enough.

I jerked back.

"Whoever's at the door," Baine shouted, "get in here now or I'm gonna shoot."

I hesitated only briefly. Not wanting Gloria shot, I raised my hands over my head and stepped into the classroom.

"Anyone else out there?" Baine asked, his rifle aimed at my chest.

Melton answered in a soothing voice. "He's the only one. I told him to wait in the hall."

"Put your weapon on the floor and kick it to me," Baine said, still focused on me.

I did as he asked, although I saw no reason to mention the handgun in my second shoulder harness.

Baine swung the rifle toward Gloria. "You! Get up here."

She stood, knees wobbling, and grimaced as though in pain as she staggered toward the front of the classroom.

I thought about making a move for my spare handgun. The moment didn't seem right. Baine was too wired. He would see me. He might react by killing Gloria.

Melton needed another chance to calm Baine down.

When Gloria reached Baine, he grabbed her arm and pulled her against him. "Is he your husband?"

She nodded, her face whitening even more. I believed she was close to passing out.

"I know your kind," Baine said, shaking her arm. "You were probably thinking about divorcing him."

"Let her go," I said. Pretending that my arms were tiring, I locked my hands behind my neck. Closer to the handgun . . .

Baine squinted at me. "Let her go? Are you insane? You're not listening to me. No one is. I'll have to do something to catch everyone's attention."

"You're wrong about no one listening," Melton said. "I'm here. You have my full attention."

Baine glanced at Melton. "You understand that what I did to that girl wasn't murder, don't you? This is war. Understand? We're all at war. Sh—she's a casualty."

"Life is indeed a struggle," Melton said.

"Tell me . . . tell me if you think I'm wrong."

Melton took another step. "Sometimes we

lose sight of what's important. We have to look inward. If we heal ourselves, then the big picture takes care of itself."

"I know what you're doing," Baine said, backpedaling toward the axe. "I can feel it. You're messing with my mind. I—I want you to stay back."

In the holding pen, a girl sobbed.

"Quiet!" Baine screamed. He fired. The bullet grazed the girl's arm and plowed into the thigh of the boy behind her.

Several students shrieked.

"I said quiet!" Baine shouted. He fired at the back wall. Shards of cinderblock flew. "Next time, someone dies."

The students quieted. One boy tore off strips from his shirt and applied them to the wounded.

"This will stop soon, one way or another," I said. "Did you know that the SBI's here? They brought a SWAT team."

"If they try to stop me, we'll all die. At least that way, my plan will get published. People will see I was right. I'll be a martyr."

"Tell me your plan," Melton said.

"No."

"Then tell me something about it. Just one little thing."

"Make divorce illegal."

"If your plan is good, people will listen," I said. "You don't need to kill people."

Baine clutched Gloria and pressed her against him, using her as a shield. "No one listens. No one! You can't fight the system from within."

"I'm not here to harm you," Melton said. "I know you sense the truth in that. Take me and threaten my life."

"I can threaten you just fine from here," Baine said.

Melton took another step. He was within four feet of Baine. "Let Gloria go. Detective Krantz will listen better if she's free."

Baine threw Gloria down and pressed the end of his rifle against her head.

Although I needed to be steady, I was unable to stop myself from trembling. The fear, the frustration, the anger were building up into uncontrollable movement.

Please, God, let Melton be close enough . . .

"N-no," Baine said thickly.

Melton exhaled and took a deep breath.

"I—I can't think," Baine said.

"Let go of your aggression," Melton whispered, taking one more step. "Find compassion in your heart."

Even from where I stood, I could sense the calming waves radiating from Melton's head. I stopped trembling.

"Nooo," Baine said, his eyes losing their focus.

Melton grimaced and clutched his chest. His head reddened. His face looked flush with fever.

"Melton, wait," I said, realizing he was absorbing Baine's anger.

"It's all right," Melton said, his voice filled with a painful rattle.

"But—"

"It's what I want."

Melon staggered, dropped to a knee, and raised his arms toward Baine.

Baine briefly aimed the rifle at me, then back at Gloria, then his eyes glazed completely. The rifle slipped from his grasp and fell to the floor.

I charged at Baine and pulled out my other handgun. Jamming it against Baine's chest, I slammed him against the chalkboard. I spun him around, twisted his arm, and pressed it against his back. "I should kill you now," I said. "But I'll get greater pleasure thinking about you rotting the rest of your life in jail."

I turned to Gloria, who had pushed herself to her feet. "Take everyone out. Use the bullhorn. Tell the SBI you're coming."

She grabbed the bullhorn and aimed it at the window. "This is Gloria Krantz. We're coming out. Jack has Baine under control."

Students ran quickly out, slowing briefly at the bottleneck at the door. The boy with the wounded thigh hobbled, his arms over the shoulders of two classmates.

"I'm staying," Gloria said.

Melton began crying and fell to his side. His fists were tight, white-knuckled. His shoulders shook.

"You okay, Melton?" I asked.

Melton opened his fists and stared at his palms. "So cruel, so wicked."

"You've overloaded yourself with Baine's aggressions," I told him. "You affected his mood, but he affected your mind. "

One of Melton's shoulders spasmed. "We met at a stress reduction seminar. Remember, Jack?" His voice weakened. "You must remember everything I've told you about peace of mind. It's important. Not just to you. To everyone. To life. Don't know how I know. But I do."

"Hang on. Paramedics will be here soon."

Melton screamed. It was a horrible sound of pain combined with the shock of realizing the seriousness of one's wounds.

The SBI burst into the room, five at first, then three more. Then the captain. "Here's Baine," I said, shoving him at the captain. Two of the SBI intercepted, though. They cuffed Baine and led him out of the classroom.

They wanted to try CPR on Melton, but I told them it was too late. He was dead. Melton had wanted peace of mind, and this was the only way he would have it.

"I'll get you to the hospital," I told Gloria.

"No need," she said.

"I insist."

I took her hand and walked toward the door. Passing the captain, I said, "In the morning, I'm resigning."

The captain opened his mouth, but said nothing, apparently not understanding how someone who had just resolved a hostage crisis could resign.

"Really?" Gloria asked, once we were in the hallway.

"We need more time together. Maybe start a family. It's time I thought about our peace of mind."

She nodded and hugged me, her tears caressing my neck. I thought about Melton, felt a warm glow of peace, and hoped it would last.

THE SIXTH DEGREE

It's like the third degree, only twice as tough....

in the hotseat D.F. LEWIS, M.F. KORN and MIKE PHILBIN

You either like the rather twisted work of D. F. Lewis and his cohorts or you don't. Being on one side or the other of that debate doesn't necessarily make you wrong; it's just that this little loose coalition of madmen write such strange, surreal work that trying to confine it to one genre or the other only dimishes its originally. Generally short, generally full of language that would make Grant Morrison's head spin, these little gems may open your mind . . . or cause you to throw a magazine across the room in frustration.

Personally, I hope you all like the likes of Lewis, Korn and Philbin, because you will be seeing quite a bit of them; their story, "Carnival Weekend," is available on the UNDER-WORLDS website (www.underworldsmagazine.com) and you will see pieces co-authored by one or more of these gentlemen in several upcoming issues (and that's not even touching upon the one story I purchased for FAN-GORIA'S FRIGHTFUL FICTION which may very well be the one story the editors at FANGO will never run due to its sheer, down and dirty sexual graphicness). Since these three men have such a strange and bizarre style, I felt they were the perfect people to subject to our own brand of interview torture, The Sixth Degree.

Each of these gentlemen were asked to choose six numbers from one to one hundred. Their choices were then cross-referenced with the master list of one hundred questions com-piled by the UNDERWORLDS Powers That Be. Neither the interviewer or interviewee knew in advance what they'd be discussing. It's interview-as-product-of-the-Id, and I guarantee you you will never hear an author discuss what he dressed up as for Halloween anywhere else….

And now, D. F. Lewis, Mike Philbin and M. F. Korn get . . . THE SIXTH DEGREE!

....

D. F. Lewis:

37: Who did you dress up as on your first Halloween?

In England in the Fifties, when I was a child, we did not, as far as I recall, celebrate Hallowe'en. Even today it is of less significance here than, say, in USA, I feel. November 5th is Guy Fawkes Day which in my youth, was very significant. We dressed up scarecrows to put on bonfires to burn. I have never dressed up on Hallowe'en, probably because I preferred the prospect of burning to death 5 days later. But never got round to it, as the novelty had worn off by then. My daughter dressed up as a witch for a party recently (she is 27). Black cloak over her jeans. Vicariously, I was that witch, too, perhaps. It's in the genes

45: What do you hope to be doing when the world comes to an end?

Selling my last copy of NENONYMOUS and calling it a success (i. e. the print magazine I run).

86: What is the most important sense to pursue your craft?

I don't actually understand fully the 'sense' there, but if it is to love writing, then I surely love my craft. (I am a writer at heart, although I have given it up for the foreseeable future).

95: Which do you prefer to write: novels or short stories?

Short stories. Vignettes. Prose poems. Novels seem to be just these things dragged out to fill a bigger space. I'm reading Proust at the moment.

12: If what Bradbury says is true about writing one million bad words before writing the first good one, when did you know you hit that millionth word?

When I encountered that word, I decided to hang up my writing boots. That millionth word was indeed a neologism I coined: 'nemonymous' (sorry to bang on about this), but I genuinely feel this word should exist, it looks real, it looks as if it has always existed, it means so much semantically and emotionally to me, it conveys the stripped down bone of existence, and this is not a novelty just hatched and ready to be worn down; it stems from an art movement I formed in 1967 called the Zeroist Group.

58: Do you feel it's important to create a 'support network' of similar artists?

Yes, and with the help of folk on Weirdmonger emailing list, I formed Wordhunger in 1999: an electronic collaborative writing venture. We currently have about 20 stories 'written' by Wordhunger now showing on the Wordhunger website. The stripped down bone of creativity.

....
Mike Philbin:

21: What's the first movie you remember seeing?

NIGHT OF THE DEMON—sound turned right

down.

22: When you were a kid, who did you dream of being?

A fireman, of course.

23: What five books would you teach in an Introduction to Literature class, and why?

The kids shouldn't be reading, it is bad for them—they may get 'ideas' and wanna go off and 'change the way we see the world'.

24: What keeps mankind alive?

Stubbornness, hunger and that little bit of piss-stinking territory he calls his own.

25: Who wrote the book of love?

Heaven 17—no, that was the "Look of Love"

(Editor's note: it shames me to write that it was actually ABC and not Heaven 17 that performed 'The Look of Love'…. my useless knowledge knows no bounds….)

99: What do you think will be the next evolutionary step of your artform?

Plug me right in, baby.
....
M. F. Korn:

7: What do you think makes your work different from others in the genre?

My writing style-how very different it is from 'mass market' prose. You as a reader either like it or hate it. But when I am collaborating, my style blends in with the other author's style. I've been told that my style is, at the very least, different.

17: Who, in your mind, is the greatest villain in the annals of literature?

It would be easy to say someone like Mr. Hyde or Dracula, but I'll say Satan, in such grande projects as Milton's PARADISE LOST. Now, I'll take that back too, and say the villian is us, the human race.

in the hotseat — M.F. KORN

29: Tell us a secret.

That Prokofiev, the famous Russian composer, as a teenager, put two oranges under his shirt on his chest and said: "Look, mama!"

72: What was the Golden Age for your genre?

Well, for both science fiction and horror, the pulp era was the Golden Age. John W. Campbell's ASTOUNDING magazine and the shudder pulps-WEIRD TALES, are the very essence of the golden age.

42: What's the most discouraging thing about practicing your craft?

Getting bad reviews, and getting novels sold, and then cancelled, the latter happening to me about 6 times.

34: Who would you wish could play you in a movie of your life?

I could be funny and say Don Knotts or Ernest Borgnine, but I'll say James Spader.

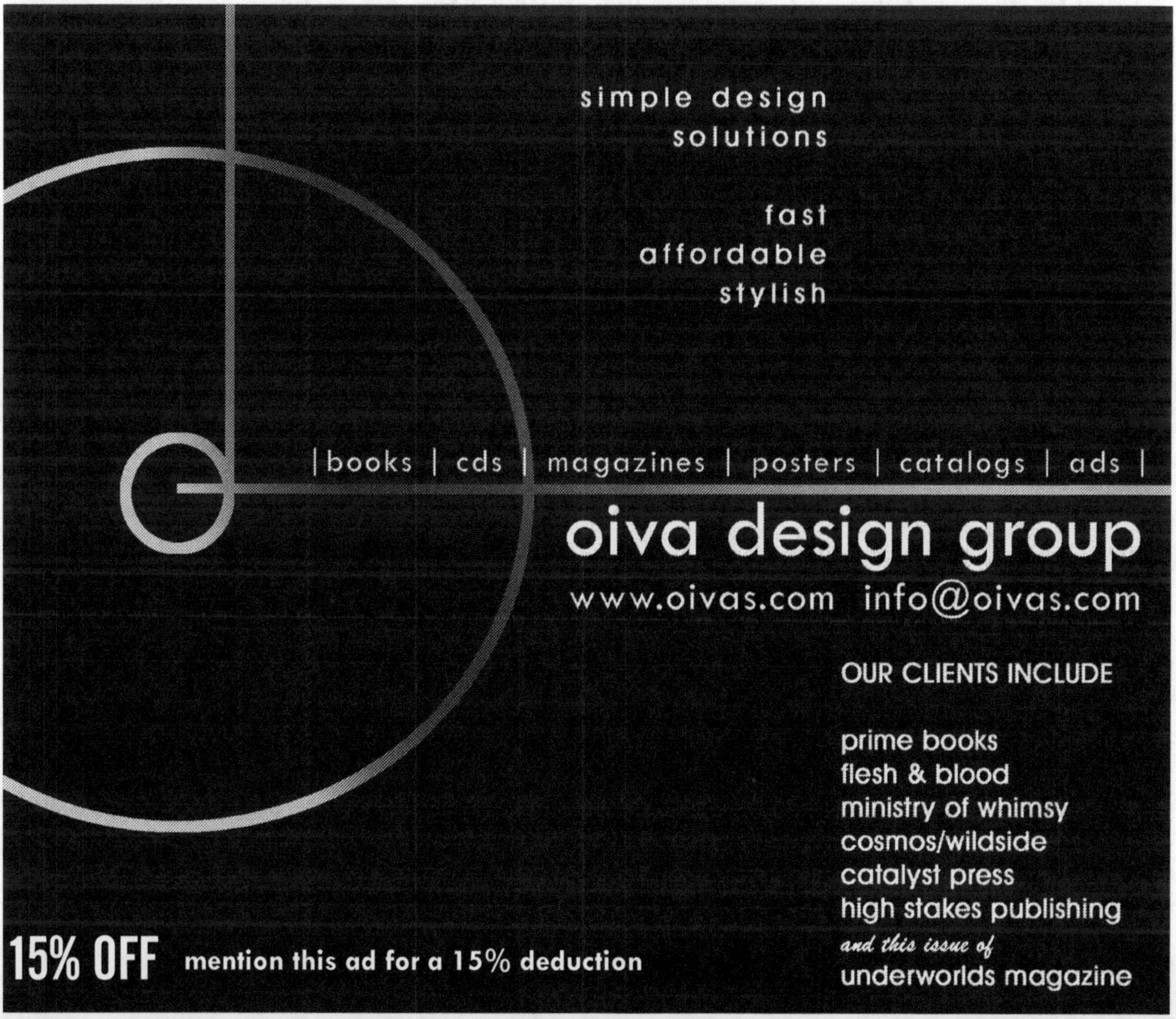

What Should I Do About That Eva Lynne?
Mark McLaughlin

That Eva Lynne!

She's a worry and a caution.

Folks say she's some kind of writer, though I dread to think what sort of made-up stories a weird old hag like that would put on paper.

I was talking to a little blonde gal who slings suds part-time down at the Bubble-Time Laundromat & Brew Pub, and she has a sister who works up at Three-Trees City Medical Center, and her brother lives across the street from that Eva Lynne, and according to him, she lives in that big blue house—blue, what a color for a house!—with three orange cats, and she drives a dark-blue car—no, let's face facts, it's a midnight-blue car.

Not what I'd call a wholesome car color. No, not at all. And orange cats? Three of them? That's just not right.

And that guy says that he has received some of her mail by mistake, and that she gets mail from places with funny stamps. Weird, faraway places in Europe.

He says that candlelight flickers in an upstairs window of her house at night—often as late as eleven!—and sometimes, he can spot some of those cats of hers sitting right there on the windowsill. Brazen as you please, for all the world to see.

My high-school girlfriend's dentist's wife works at the Three-Trees City Library, and she says that sometimes that Eva Lynne will check out up to five or six books at a time. And not just paperbacks—we're talking books with spines and dust-jackets. And wait until you hear this: some of those books are what they call science-fiction, and others are all about what folks do in foreign lands.

That Eva Lynne! A person's got to keep a cautious eye on a woman like that. Think about it - an old woman who lives in a blue house who likes orange cats. And candlelight. And midnight-blue cars. A woman who reads big thick science-fiction books and writes made-up stories and gets letters from folks who ain't from around here.

What's her scheme?

Plus, her full name is Eva Lynne Stedman. I don't want to freak you out or cause undue alarm, but I will tell you this! I live in my Grandma's spare room and one day, after I got done playing Scrabble with Grandma—she won, by the way—I remembered something from some scary movie I'd seen once—it was either ROSEMARY'S BABY or one of them "Chucky" killer-doll shows. Whichever one it was, it said something about witches having names that spell other things when you rearrange the letters. So I spelled out EVA LYNNE STEDMAN with those little wooden pieces and then I started moving around the letters, and you know what? They spelled out EVYL DEMAN STANNE.

I'll write down the letters for you.

See? The words kind of look like EVIL DEMON STAIN, and I think that pretty much sums up the whole deal! That woman, that Eva Lynne, is clearly an evil demon stain on Three-Trees City.

After I saw those terrifying Scrabble letters, I said to myself, "What should I do about that Eva Lynne?"

And so, that's why I've been sending her all that hate mail and making those anonymous calls, Officer. But how was I to know that sneaky old hag had caller ID? Yeah, I've been trying to drive her right out of town.

But why am I the one being punished? What I was doing should count as a community service.

She's the evil one, Officer. The demon. The stain.

Not me. 

CLARK ASHTON SMITH
and the Bohemian Club

~ DERRICK M. HUSSEY ~

Clark Ashton Smith (1893-1961) is best known today as a contributor of fantastic tales of horror to *Weird Tales* in the 1930s. In his teens, under the tutelage of the poet laureate of the west coast, George Sterling (1869-1926), Smith had found a large measure of success as a poet. His first book of poetry, *The Star-Treader and Others* (1912) was hailed as the work of a prodigy. In 1913, Smith participated in a theatrical production at the midsummer retreat of the legendary Bohemian Club of San Francisco.

Smith received his introduction to the Bohemian Club through Sterling, a long-time member. In his last years Sterling lived at the Club full-time, and it was there that Sterling killed himself by poison before his fifty-seventh birthday. Started "for the promotion of good fellowship among journalists and the elevation of journalism to that place in the proper estimation to which it is entitled," the Bohemian Club ultimately extended membership to artists of all kinds, and purchased a plot of undeveloped land for recreational purposes.

This area, the Grove, is a forested plot owned by the Club for over a century and located on the Russian River, sixty-five miles north of San Francisco. For three weekends every summer the club's members and their guests gather for the "Midsummer Jinks." Highlights of this conclave include a series of almost ritualistic activities, such as a bonfire called the Cremation of Care, as well as theatrical presentations. Simple skits are called Low Jinks, while the High

Jinks center upon the Grove Plays, for which original plays and special music is written, and unique costumes and scenery designed, for a solitary presentation.

The tradition of Grove Plays at the Midsummer Jinks began in 1902. Most of the plays over the next several years were based generally upon historical or mythological characters and texts. However, George Sterling and others shortly began to draft wholly imaginary, fantastic plays for the club. The Grove Play for 1913, "The Fall of Ug: A Masque of Fear," by Rufus Steele, falls resoundingly into the fantastic category. The souvenir program for this performance lists "C. A. Smith" as a Shepherd.

The plot of "The Fall of Ug" goes somewhat as follows. A young prince and his hunting companions follow a stag through a forest on Mid-Summer Day. They pause before a colossal stone figure of Ug, the God of Fear, which has long blocked the white path leading Heavenward up the hill. The people, it develops, come here this very night for the annual human sacrifice to Ug, Husbandmen, Shepherds, Huntsmen, Warriors, King, High Priest, Prince, Jester, Scribe, Nobles, Lords—the entire world, in fact—arrive and in a mighty chorus voice their trembling tribute to the god. Smith's few scenes onstage took place early in the play, when the Shepherds arrived on the scene to praise Ug. While they enter, each carrying a live lamb (!) and bearing a crook, they are singing the Song of the Shepherds:

Mid meadows sweet with Grasses,
Through sylvan shadows cool
The flock serenely passes
To rest beside the pool.
No lamb is left to wander
Upon the hillside steep;
The wolf is watching yonder,
The shepherd guards his sheep.

After the song is sung, Smith and the other Shepherds dispose themselves upon the ground, presumably guarding their sheep. Later in the play, the High Priest commands the Shepherds to bow before Ug's form. No longer mindful of their charges, they fling down their lambs, which run bleating offstage! Making "the Sign of Ug," whatever that means, and showing grave agitation, the Shepherds kneel. The Jester, meanwhile, has climbed to an eminence from which he mocks the Shepherds with this couplet:

Oh, See our frightened Shepherds bow and weep:
They are as bold as any newborn sheep!

For most of the Shepherds, all that remained wass to sing the lengthy Song of Ug with the rest of the company. However, two men from each walk of life represented are later named as Ug's "Protectors." The two Shepherds named are Tord and Kim; unfortunately, the souvenir book does not specify the actors' names. Tord and Kim were significantly involved in several other scenes.

At the end of the play, predictably, Ug is overthrown. Uttering a prayer saves the Prince, who was named as Ug's sacrifice. Then, "in the noise and mystery of a convulsion," Ug is dimly seen to shrivel and go down into utter nothingness. It remains a mystery how the destruction of Ug was effected onstage. A photograph of one scene of the play shows Ug to have been a towering beaked entity, probably tent-like and thus easily collapsible. The photograph also shows a group of people massed before Ug, and it is likely that Clark Ashton Smith is among them, although the photograph is too small to be certain.

Smith never felt entirely comfortable with the San Francisco literati, being more apolitical than most. Smith's stepson, William Dorman, expressed amazement that Smith was ever at the Bohemian Grove. Still, for a time Smith evidently felt secure in the merits of his work and safe in the company of his friend and mentor. After releasing several more books of poetry, at the encouragement of H. P. Lovecraft he began writing fiction for the pulp magazines of the era. Increasingly disgusted with commercial writing, however, Smith later focused again on poetry, but by the 1950s had virtually ceased writing altogether. In his later years he was known to some as an eccentric, living on the margins of society. Perhaps his early taste of fame, and the experience of fellowship with the elite, made his becoming a virtual pariah all the more bitterly felt. Certainly many of the characters in his mature tales are outsiders with a cynical view of society.

Presently, Smith's work is enjoying a renaissance. Already, the twenty-first century has seen the release of no less than five books of his fiction, poetry and collected letters. A full-scale biography, long overdue, is nearing completion. Two separate historical markers have been erected in his native town of Auburn, California. Clark Ashton Smith's participation in the Grove Play for 1913 forms but a brief chapter in his long life. Nevertheless, it is a significant one. For a youth barely twenty, catapulted into the limelight with the recognition of poetry, mingling with the powerful and famous, and escorted by the most important poet in the California scene, it must have been a heady time indeed.

THE FEMALE OF THE SPECIES
Megan Powell

When I got into work, everybody was taking bets on how long it would take Gundersen to get a confession. I put a few bucks down on fifteen minutes, because Gundersen's pretty damn good at interrogation. It's the eyes, nice and flat and reptilian, rather than the threat of force (or use of force), because Gundersen actually looks pretty wimpy.

After I'd placed my bet, my partner Greg filled me in on the case. Arnold Haskins had been found stabbed to death in his house. Ten years after the happiest day of their lives, he and his wife Marianne were estranged. She'd been stepping out, he'd found out, and in any case the marriage had been over for years . . . So said not-quite-ex-wifey, who also said they'd been going to counseling. That didn't quite match with the marriage being dead, but once Greg gave me a picture of Arnold's assets I appreciated Marianne's motivation.

Gundersen was talking to the estranged wife. Or rather, subjecting the estranged wife to The Stare. Fifteen minutes suddenly seemed like an awful long time; she was looking pretty teary already, and I kissed my money goodbye. Gundersen's partner had the boyfriend in a separate room. Jeff Varney does look like he can kick your ass, though I'm almost positive that last excessive force charge was bogus.

"So smart money says it was the wife?" I asked Greg. "Or are you hoping they don't know the Prisoner's Dilemma?"

The Prisoner's Dilemma is simple. You've got two co-conspirators in separate rooms, and a sweet deal on the table. The first to confess gets the sweet deal, and the other guy gets screwed. If they both confess, they get reduced sentences—not the sweet deal, but not the max either. But if they both manage to keep their mouths shut, they get off scot free. It's basically a big trust exercise.

In my experience, estranged wives and their new boyfriends don't typically do too well at trust exercises.

"Smart money says it was at least the wife," Greg said. "The female of the species is more deadly than the male."

Deadly or not, Marianne Haskins was sobbing. Maybe it was an act, maybe not. Her husband's body hadn't been cold when she and her boyfriend were hauled in, so it would be tough to tell if hormone-induced hysterics were related to committing the crime or finding out that it had happened and being accused of murder.

The boyfriend was doing a little better, now at the mostly pissed stage. But he seemed to be trying to control his angry outbursts, with Varney doing his big mean black guy glare across the table from him. Varney's glare doesn't quite warrant capitalization, but it might after he's had a couple more years to refine it.

"How do we stand on evidence?"

"We found the murder weapon. One of those little screwdrivers," Greg told me. "It was wrapped up in a bloody rag and flushed down the boyfriend's toilet. The plumbing backed up—not much fun for the guys who retrieved it, but at least they don't have to go pound the pavement and turn over a few hundred garbage cans."

"Lucky them," I frowned.

I watched the two interrogations for another couple of minutes. One of them really should have caved in by now. I got a little apprehensive. The murderer might have planned to hide behind the innocent one, figuring that our evidence against them would be equally incriminating, but specific to neither. If they'd both been in on it, maybe they knew about the Prisoner's Dilemma.

In either case, Gundersen and Varney were getting into a rut. What we needed was some new evidence—or, failing that, a new perspective.

I excused myself to the ladies room, and after a minute came back and knocked on Varney's door. He looked a little annoyed at me for messing up his routine, but he also seemed aware he was hitting a wall and let me in. "Detective Mills," he said by way of greeting and introduction, then let me have the chair and loomed behind me.

"Hello, Tom," I said. "Do you mind if I call you Tom?"

Tom Womack shrugged, looking only moderately less pissed at me than at Varney.

"My partner filled me in on this case," I said. "Dead husband, murder weapon found at the boyfriend's apartment where the wife frequently stayed. We'll convict at least one of you. It'd be nice if we convicted the murderer, but we'll take what we can get."

Womack scowled. "I already told you, I didn't do it. And Marianne wouldn't. She's not that sort of person."

But he wasn't giving her an absolute alibi. No doubt Varney made a mental note of that as well. "You'd be surprised what people do. Or maybe not. I don't know who killed Arnold Haskins. But I know who didn't dispose of the murder weapon."

Womack frowned in confusion. I pulled out the Sanibag I'd taken from the ladies room and slapped it down on the table.

"If there's one thing every woman's taught from the day she gets her first period, it's that you can't flush things down the toilet."

Womack was staring at the Sanibag and seemed to be having difficulty breathing. It hadn't even taken hard evidence to demoralize him. I savored the expression on his face for a moment.

"You can't flush pads, you can't flush tampons and you can't flush murder weapons. Women know that. Plumbers know that. Reasonably intelligent people know that. Dumb boyfriends don't. If you want my advice, start talking."

With that, I stood up and left the room. Varney settled back into his chair; I figured he could pick up on my momentum and get either a confession or some quality finger-pointing.

I was greeted by applause, and I sketched a little bow. "My condolences on losing the bet," Greg said.

I shrugged. "This was more fun. I did my part to help get a confession, and I proved you wrong."

"How so?"

"The female of the species is more intelligent than the male."

LIFE'S LOSER / NICHOLAS KNIGHT

Donald threw the smoking gun into the river, hopped into his car, and sped off into the night.

After driving for a couple of blocks, his nervousness faded, quickly replaced by elation. He felt triumphant. Vindicated! Never again would he have to listen to Mikey gloat, or be embarrassed by Mikey's put-downs.

*****

Everything Donald had ever done, Mikey had copied . . . and had done better. "Nice try, loser," was what Donald had always heard.

It had all started one Halloween back in elementary school. Donald had been the first one in the class to think of dressing up like a robot, but he'd made the mistake of telling Mikey about his costume. On Halloween, Mikey made sure to arrive at school first . . . wearing a robot costume of his own. The children all thought Mikey's costume was amazing, what with the beeping control panel in his chest and multiple working blender attachments where his hands should be. Donald's costume was almost as impressive, but no one paid him any attention—Mikey took all the glory.

And so it had continued from there on out. Mikey had beaten him in sports. Mikey had scored higher grades. Mikey had won the hearts of all the girls Donald had ever been interested in. Mikey had gotten the better jobs. And he'd always rubbed it in Donald's face: "Nice try, loser."

Then tonight, twenty years after that first fateful Halloween party, the two "friends" were out at another party, and once again Mikey had copied Donald's costume. This time, they were both dressed as Devils. Their costumes were so similar, that Donald's girlfriend apparently hadn't realized that she'd snuck into the host's guest bedroom for a sexual tryst with the wrong Devil.

Donald felt that Mikey had gone too far, and he decided to put an end to their rivalry once and for all. When Mikey went outside for a smoke, Donald followed him. After he pulled the trigger, Donald got to have what he'd always wanted—the final word. "Who's the loser now?" he'd sneered at his dead friend.

*****

Speeding around a bend, Donald didn't see the red light until it was too late. He hit the brakes and his tires squealed in protest as his car hurled into the intersection. He was hit from both sides. The car exploded before the paramedics could get the unconscious driver out.

Donald found himself in purgatory. A demon roughly escorted him to the Gates of Hell, where the Devil stood waiting. Donald quickly realized that it wasn't *the* Devil standing there; it was Mikey, still dressed in his convincing costume.

But something wasn't right—Mikey was fading in and out of sight.

Seeing Donald, Mikey smiled. "The paramedics just got to my body, they're reviving me . . . Nice try, loser!"

The PERSISTENCE OF DREAMS

MONICA J. O'ROURKE

The same faces: living skeletons covered in rags and filth, reaching out to her, to one another. Shared quarters never graced by sunlight save for the pale haze feathering through the slats in the windowless walls. The floors: dirt, the bunk beds splintered planks covered by a tattered blanket.

Always the same dream.

Sydney sat up in the darkness and found the bottle of Xanax. Swallowed a pill, a habit-forming bullet that was supposed to be used as a last resort.

Like during a panic attack.

Settled back into the pillows. Relived the dream, played it out in her mind. The soldiers barking commands at the half-dead masses, striking them with guns or fists, kicking them with steel-tipped boots. Lining up the bony carcasses to butcher in the slush or in the mud.

Later in her therapist's office, she again mentioned her interest in trying Regression Therapy.

Dr. Alden dismissed the idea. "It's anxiety, Sydney, not reincarnation. You're usually pragmatic about these things."

"Why can't we try it?"

"You're already convinced that you know the answers. Your unconscious mind is blocking you and will continue to block you until you're ready to accept the cause of your anxiety."

Dr. Alden crossed her arms over her small chest. "I believe your dreams are part of a much bigger problem. And since this is a recurring dream, I think you're stuck, unable to progress. Dreaming of victims, no less. We've talked about your sexual abuse as a child . . ."

Sydney shook her head. "I don't know that I was abused. I have no real memory of it."

"This might be what you're looking for. Perhaps your mind is ready to let you in."

After a moment of silence, Sydney said, "I'd like to try hypnosis. I've been having those dreams for months now. It feels like someone's trying to communicate with me. I know it sounds crazy, but—"

"You've seen *Schindler's List* too many times. It's the foundation of your fantasies, something your mind has grasped as a common idea. You equate your being a victim with the Holocaust, and your mind has filled in the blanks."

"But—"

"Time's up for today. See you next week. Need a refill on your meds?"

Old-fashioned newsreels showed Nazi atrocities in black and white, but her dreams were visions in contrasting colors. Rust-hued tattered cloth remnants hanging from ruined bodies. Grays and blues and yellows of battered and abused flesh.

In the dreams, people talked to her, interacted with her. She smelled the suffering and despair, shared their desperation.

"Don't be afraid," she whispered to a cowering living-dead woman. Her own words were foreign, spoken in a language she'd never learned yet somehow understood.

"*Raus*," a guard barked, bodies pouring out the barracks door like fetid water.

The guard said to Sydney, "*Was hast du da drin gemacht?*"

She didn't understand. "I'm sorry . . ."

The guard's face was fever-flushed in anger. "I asked what you were doing in there. Are you deaf?"

She didn't answer.

"*Geh!*" He pointed toward the courtyard and shoved her into the crowd.

"I'm telling you," Sydney cried, collapsing into the overstuffed office chair. "The dreams are -- they're not like dreams."

"What are they like?" Dr. Alden asked, leaning forward.

"It's like I'm there. I can . . . feel their pain. I—" She swallowed. "Can smell the . . . their blood. The fear. They scream. Always screaming. Cries for help. I hear them, begging for their babies . . . Then the gunshots. But the screams. Always the screams."

"Go on."

"That's it." Sydney palmed away tears. "Except this time a guard spoke to me. *Geh*, he said. And I knew what he meant."

"Just because you understood one word doesn't mean anything. Especially such an obvious one. You could have figured it out from his body language."

"It was more than just one—"

"Where did he want you to go?"

"To the yard with the others."

"You heard babies."

"Yes," Sydney said wistfully. "Innocent babies."

"Like the one you gave up?"

"No. Not like that," she snapped.

"Are you sure?"

Sydney didn't have anything to add.

"Are you dressed?"

"What?"

"In your Nazi dream," Dr. Alden said. "What are you wearing? Are you dressed like everyone else? Are you cold?"

Sydney thought for a moment. "I don't know. I don't remember being cold."

"I've been researching your dreams. I thought Freud or Jung would've had something to say about this. But I haven't found anything yet. I have a call in to a colleague as well."

Sydney examined the fabric pattern on the chair arm, occasionally glancing at the doctor.

"Don't worry, Sydney, I'm still looking. I haven't given up." She smiled, a look Sydney guessed was supposed to be comforting but was unnerving instead.

"Do you think now we could try hypnosis now? Or Regression Therapy?"

"Honestly, Sydney. Are you still on that kick? I wish I could get you to understand . . . Past life regression is another name for something called confabulation. A mixture of your own experiences coupled with a vivid imagination. And reincarnation? It's crap. It's your own mind recalling events from your life and your imagination. You have to deal with the *now*, Sydney. Stop looking for miracle answers because they don't exist. You'll just end up getting hurt."

"I get the point," Sydney muttered. "You don't have to be so damned blunt. Obviously I won't change your mind."

"No you won't. I don't believe in it, and I think it could end up being harmful. That type of therapy introduces all sorts of elements into an already fragile mind. Just leave it alone. You'll remember things when you need to."

Alden looked at the clock. "See you next week."

"My psychiatrist believes this is a waste of time, that it's nonsense. She said it was something made up of your own imagination."

"Confabulation." Dr. Morris offered a small smile. "What do you think?"

"I don't know. I have these vivid dreams about a concentration camp, where everyone speaks several languages. Somehow I understand them, even though I don't know any language other than English."

Dr. Morris scribbled as Sydney talked, his only acknowledgement a constant head bobbing, his fleshy neck wobbling.

"The dreams are so real. More like memories. I feel like this is another part of my life. Or maybe another life altogether. Does that make any sense?"

He wrote for a few more seconds before looking up from the notepad and leaned back in his chair. "Actually, it doesn't sound like reincarnation. Past Life Regression Therapy is normally used to treat fears or phobias. Finding out what might have occurred in another life or another time, and seeing how it affects your present day self.

"I didn't get that impression from your intake interview. Your dreams are not affecting your life, at least in a tangible way. Clearly you're upset about them, but you haven't developed any sort of condition because of them. It sounds like the dreams might be a manifestation of another trauma, perhaps something from your childhood you've repressed."

Sydney shook her head. "That's what my shrink says."

"Reincarnation doesn't normally manifest through dreams, not alone anyway. A dream would be a symptom, not the event itself."

"Then what can I do?"

"I would normally suggest a dream therapist, but your pattern of dreams suggest something more. The way you interact for example, almost as if you're bringing something back with you. And you seem convinced a past life, or an alternate life, is trying to communicate with you."

Sydney nodded and she met the strong gaze of his coffee colored eyes. "That's right. Like someone is trying to tell me something."

"I'd like to try Regression Therapy. We might discover your concentration camp dreams are a metaphor for something else in your life. It might not be about past lives at all, but something about your current life."

"Yes, you've mentioned that."

"I want to make sure you understand. I'm not promising you anything." He leaned forward into the desk and folded his arms on the blotter. "Since most people equate the Holocaust with something evil, perhaps your experiences in this concentration camp represents something bad in your life. Something bad that happened to you. Or something you did that you felt was evil."

"Evil? I haven't done anything evil."

"I'm not accusing you of anything. But your unconscious mind might be."

The silence felt as thick as congealing blood.

Dr. Morris cleared his throat. "Ready to begin?"

She felt defeated, even victimized. "I guess so."

He walked across the room and pulled down the shade. The windowsill was cluttered with lush plants, with too many frames filled with happy, grinning children and harried-looking adults, too many *chotchkes*. He pushed aside the clutter and planted his fleshy hips on the sill.

"I want you to be comfortable with this."

Her nails were imbedded in the armchair's fabric.

"We're going to come up with a signal, something to indicate to me that you're too uncomfortable to continue. Something simple. If you need to stop, raise your right thumb."

She relaxed her shoulders, nodded.

He led her to the sofa. When he returned to his desk, he turned on the tape recorder. "Lean back or lie down. Whatever you're comfortable with."

She sank into the overstuffed cushions.

"Okay, Sydney. Close your eyes. Are you comfortable?"

She nodded.

"You can answer me."

"Yes." Her muscles relaxed, the tension in her shoulders and neck relinquishing their grip.

"I'm going to relax you more completely. In a moment I'm going to begin counting backwards from ten to one. The moment I say the number ten your eyelids will remain closed. In your mind's eye you'll see yourself at the top of a small set of stairs."

She could picture the stairs; she was at her grandmother's house at the beach, and she could taste the saltwater lingering in the air.

"The moment I say the number nine, and each additional number, you will move down those stairs, relaxing more completely. At the base of the stairs is a large feather bed, with a comfortable feather pillow. The moment I say the number one you will sink into that bed and rest your head on that feather pillow."

Her grandmother had a feather bed, and it was there that—

Slowly she descended the steps as he counted down, pictures on the stairwell walls that looked like they belonged in an antique shop. Pictures of relatives dead for many years. And pictures of relatives Sydney wished were dead.

She felt herself slipping away, the bed's feathery softness embracing her, quills poking through the coverlet.

"Three . . . breathe in deeply . . . Two . . . On the next number, number one, simply sink into that bed, become more calm, more peaceful, more relaxed. One . . . Sinking . . . let every muscle go limp and loose as you sink into a more calm, peaceful state."

Sydney was aware of her surroundings. The feathers tickled her, and the waves crashed onto the shoreline outside the bedroom window.

"Can you hear me, Sydney?"

"Yes," she muttered, too relaxed to speak any louder.

"We're going back now. Back to the place in your dreams. We're in the concentration camp now. Can you see it? Are you there?"

She said softly, "I'm in the camp." She took Dr. Morris with her.

In the Medical Building, wandering through leaking corridors, naked bulbs suspended from threadbare cords. Her breath billowed passage, and her footfalls echoed as she turned corners.

Hollow eyes begged for help from tables in rooms with doors ajar. Hands outstretched, mouths twisted in hideous parody of smiles.

Instead of helping, she wandered further, discovered the source of the arctic cold, colder even than the frigid temperatures outside.

Sydney entered the room.

Inside, an oversized glass tank, large enough to hold several people. Two men and one woman were naked and submerged up to their necks in the water.

Sydney stole a glance at the temperature gauge. The water measured fifteen degrees.

The three subjects were tethered to the side of the tank. They struggled in the water, tried to reach one another. Tried to pull their arms around their bodies for warmth. Icicles had formed on their wet heads, on the mucus trickling from their noses. Breath puffed in front of their faces like a wall of fog.

An alarm sounded and they were pulled from the water and wrapped in blankets.

They began to scream as their limbs thawed, as their frozen and frostbitten bodies rapidly warmed to the temperature of the room. Doctors tended to the subjects while others scribbled on clipboards.

One of the men was thrown back into the tank like an undersized fish, screaming as he hit the water. His flesh was bleached white from the icy cold, but his fingers and toes had blackened, inevitably gangrenous. His heart imploded from the shock, every orifice trickling fluids as he floated facedown in the pool.

Mesmerized, Sydney stared. Flooded with

awe, wondered what the results of the tests looked like . . .

"Sydney, you need to come back now. Do you understand?"

She nodded.

"I want you to bring back only what will help you. I want you to leave behind the bad feelings, bring back only what you need. Do you understand?"

Again she nodded.

"I'm going to count from one to five, and then I'll say, 'Fully aware'. At the count of five, your eyes are open, and you are then fully aware, feeling calm, refreshed, relaxed."

Her breathing was an easy rhythm.

"One, you're returning to full awareness. Two, each muscle and nerve in your body is loose and limp and relaxed. Three, you're feeling perfect in every way, emotionally calm and serene.

"On the number four, your eyes begin to feel sparkling clear. Eyelids open. Five, fully aware now, feeling rested, full of energy. Take a good, deep breath, fill up your lungs."

Her eyelids popped open. "What happened?"

"Tell me what you remember."

She rubbed here eyes. "A medical building. Torture. Experiments in water. What did I say?"

"I'm not sure. It wasn't English. You ignored my questions and became angry when I tried to stop the session."

"I don't remember that."

"I've never seen anything like this," he said. "You say you've never studied a foreign language?"

"No. Was it German?"

"I think so. I need to get this tape translated." He flitted around his office like a germinating insect, tossing items into his briefcase. "This is really something. I can't wait to see what this is."

"You don't know?"

"Well no, not yet."

"What do I do now?"

"Do?"

"The dreams. I haven't been able to sleep. What am I supposed to do? This session doesn't seem to have helped."

"Let me see what's on the tape. Maybe there's something there that can help. I'll get back to you, Sydney. I have a friend who works in languages at NYU. In the meantime, try chamomile tea, and avoid spicy foods. That should help you sleep better."

He directed her out of his office. "I'm sorry I don't have any answers for you yet, but this was just one session, after all."

"Wait—" But he was gone, and she was left standing in the street, surrounded by commuters fighting their way home, yet feeling utterly alone.

Sydney curled up on the sofa with a bowl of soup and a Grisham novel and tried to unwind. Bits of dream remnants haunted her, as if they were somehow trying to take control.

Snuggling into the cushions, she stretched out along the length of the couch and fell asleep.

Light snow had fallen, giving the landscaped grayness of the barbed-wire-enclosed compound a paradoxical white layer of purity.

Gunshots. Screams. Sydney stood beside dozens of prisoners lined naked in the snow.

Commands barked in English, German, Polish. Prisoners were instructed to drop to their knees. One by one, systematically shot, one bullet per prisoner, close range in the head. Only it was *every other prisoner*. Survivors shook and screamed as they were spared, cowering beside dead relatives and friends.

They knelt in the freezing snow, consumed by grief and despair.

"You!" A young guard stormed over, aimed his pistol point-blank at Sydney. Fury on his face. He cocked the hammer.

Her eyes flew open. Tugged on her shirt, yanked it away from her throat, gasped for air. Fumbled in the dark for the phone. She punched in Dr. Alden's memorized number and blurted a message for the answering service to call the doctor.

The Xanax bottle was on the coffee table, and she swallowed a pill. When the phone rang, Sydney screamed into it. "They're trying to kill me!"

"What? Who is?"

"In my dream," she sobbed.

"Calm down, Sydney. Take a Xanax."

"I did." She wiped the back of her hand under her nose, her face wet with tears and mucus. "I'm scared."

"Deep breaths. Relax, Sydney. You're safe."

"No I'm not! I can't go back to sleep. He'll kill me!"

"I'm calling an ambulance for you, and I'll meet you at Mount Sinai. Okay?"

Sydney nodded.

"Sydney? Okay?"

"Yes," she sobbed. "Okay." She dropped the phone onto the couch and pulled her knees up to her chest.

She wouldn't let them give her anything to help her sleep. The Xanax had relaxed her too much already. Her eyes were heavy and burning and she fought to keep them open.

Dr. Alden pulled up a chair.

Sydney's room was antiseptic and was a strange fusion of smells—lingering bleach and ammonia and a not-fresh tang of old homeless men who didn't like to bathe. A lingering scent of despair, reserved for those like Sydney who could appreciate it.

"What happened, Sydney? You were doing so well."

She wanted to spit in Alden's face. Sydney got the feeling her shrink was annoyed at being woken up and dragged out of bed in the middle of the night.

"I had another dream." Sat up, propped two flat pillows behind her back. "A guard aimed a gun at me, said 'you'."

"What else?"

"What else? Nothing else. He was aiming a gun at me!"

Dr. Alden rubbed her hands together as if warming them. "Did anything else happen?"

Sydney closed her eyes. "People were being shot. But not all of them. Just every other one."

"What else?"

Sydney looked at her. "Nothing."

"Something must have triggered this. What have you done differently lately?"

Sydney cleared her throat. "I went under hypnosis."

"When were you planning on sharing that with me? Still wondering why you've had an attack? Do you know what sort of damage can be caused by going to some quack?"

"You don't even know who I went to. I spoke in a foreign language. He got it all on tape."

"Listen to me. *These are nothing but dreams.* What's happening to you can be explained, but you have to listen to me. You have to trust me."

She buried her face in her palms. "Why won't you believe me? If I go to sleep, I'm dead!"

Dr. Alden leaned back, her chair protesting the shift in weight. She rubbed her bloodshot eyes. "What do you plan to do, never sleep again?"

"If I have to." She chewed on a cuticle.

Dr. Alden stood up. "I need some sleep. Maybe you can go without, but I can't." She headed toward the door. "Please try to get some rest. I promise you'll be fine."

Bleary-eyed, hair disheveled, Sydney snapped open her drooping lids.

"Why won't you eat, Sydney?"

She glared at her shrink. "Food can be drugged. I've eaten apples and crackers from the vending machine. I only drink soda from the machines and water from the sink. I don't think you can drug that. I know you want me to sleep but you can't make me."

Dr. Alden shook her head. "You sound like a

spoiled child. And you're a mess. Have you seen yourself?"

Sydney shook her head. "I don't give a shit."

"How long do you think you can keep this up, this not sleeping? How long do you think the human body can go without sleep?"

Sydney turned away, interested in her toenail. "I'm only worried about now."

"You won't last more than a week. Your body won't let you. Let's talk about this now, this destructive behavior."

"I don't want to talk about anything."

"You'd just started talking about being molested. I think we need to discuss that further."

"No," Sydney snapped. "It makes no goddamn difference, don't you see? My getting molested by some fucked up relative has nothing to do with my dreams. Why won't you believe me? If I go to sleep I'll never wake up."

"You feel guilty for what happened to you as a child, and you're acting it out in your dreams. This happens to abuse victims. It's a defense mechanism. You're the victim all over again."

"It's not like that. The dreams are real."

"It *is* like that. Dreams are part of your unconscious. They're not real. A dream can't hurt you."

Sydney began to weep. "What if you're wrong?"

"I'm not."

"But what if they try to kill me? What if-"

"They won't, Sydney. Listen to me. No one has ever died from a dream."

"How do you know?" She wiped away her tears with her fingers and pushed the hair off her forehead.

Dr. Alden smiled. "Come on. Get some sleep. I'll stay with you."

Sydney scrunched down in the bed, too exhausted to offer any further resistance.

"If I suspect you're in any trouble at all, I'll wake you."

She woke twelve hours later. Shortly after, the doctor on duty came in to take her pulse. "Dr. Alden's on her way to see you. She was pleased to hear you survived the night."

Sydney smiled. "I didn't have any dreams."

"Sure you did. We all dream, all night long. We just don't remember most of them. If we didn't dream, we'd go insane. Studies have been done on dream deprivation. People can't survive without dreaming." He jotted her pulse on her chart and left.

She thought about a taunt from her childhood. Her sister, angry that Sydney had broken her favorite doll, warned her that everything balanced out in the end. Her sister punched her in the arm and told her that God would punish her for being such an evil girl.

Sydney didn't think the universe was punishing her with dream torture because of a broken doll. Or even because of her broken marriage. But she wondered if this might be justice for her decision to give up the baby she'd been carrying.

She tried to relax, hoped her sleep would come as easily when she was discharged from the hospital. Sleep finally came, but then someone shook her shoulder, yelled for her to get up. Why was the nurse screaming at her?

"What's wrong with you?" the soldier barked.

Her surroundings came into focus. Back inside the camp. Chills seized her bowels. Her stomach roiled.

"Here." The guard pointed the gun at her chest.

Startled, she stepped back.

"Take it," he snapped, thrusting it at her.

"What?

"Idiot. I don't know what's wrong with you. Just take it."

She reached out, and he slapped the pistol into her palm.

"Let's go," he said, but she stood there and stared at the gun in her outstretched hands.

"Move!"

She ran after him.

Hundreds of people, standing or sitting in the snow, bare feet with blackened toes, raw blistered skin exposed to the wind. Tattered clothing flapped in the icy breeze. They huddled together, desperately searching for warmth from bodies too thin to produce any decent amount of heat. A small group, off to the side, singing in Hebrew, offering their smiles to the heavens.

Sydney stared into the crowds and they stared back at her, some *through* her.

What were they staring at? This wasn't her fault. Who were *they* to be judgmental? Studied the dying faces, at human skeletons, skin pulled taut over bone and blood vessels. Their plight was becoming tiresome.

"This one," a guard said, pulling her arm. "Here."

Sydney followed.

The guard stopped beside a young girl on her knees. "This is the one. The thief. She stole food from the dead. Shoot her."

Sydney looked at the guard, at the gun. Glanced at the uniform warming her body, at the black boots, felt a beard on her strong, masculine face.

"You've been slagging off. Do it or go on report."

She lifted the gun, cocked it. Her hand shook. She bit the inside of her cheek.

"She's a goddamn *Jew*, "he spat. "Do it."

Weeping into her hands as if trying to capture the life force of her tears In her cupped palms. A girl whose only crime had been her religion, her only sin starvation.

But Sydney raised the gun and aimed it at the child's head. Felt a bizarre surge of strength from the guard she shared her body with. Felt his hatred. Wondered if he dreamed about her, shared her life the way she shared his, the way she dreamed about this other life.

Even if this was a dream, this felt right. Felt like destiny. Her destiny. That's what the dreams

had been telling her. They weren't a warning, they were an invitation.

The girl wasn't an innocent, she was a Jew. *Jew.*

The word coursed through her mind like poison. She shared the hatred this man felt. Her face hardened, lips pulled into a sneer.

Her index finger pulled the trigger.

The girl's blood and brains coated her hands, spattered their face and clothes.

Within minutes, the camp was swarming with American soldiers. Pandemonium erupted. They had broken into the compound and were freeing prisoners.

Sydney dropped the pistol.

The prisoners swarmed, liberated at last from their torture. The Americans rounded up the guards.

Prisoners attacked while the American soldiers looked the other way. Screams were heard throughout the camp, anguished cries mingled with joy from the Jewish survivors, fresh screams of pain and despair from the German guards.

Sydney was attacked by a mob and knocked to the ground. Weak, malnourished, abused skeletons pounded on her, the Nazi soldier. They'd found new strength in their anger and kicked and punched Sydney and the other guards until their bones were powder, until their cartilage was sponge.

Cowered on the ground, eyes swollen shut, countless broken bones jutted from broken skin, Sydney curled Into a ball. Pleaded for mercy, begged the Americans to save her.

Liberated prisoners tied ropes around her arms and played tug-of-war.

She tried to understand what she'd done in her other life to deserve this.

Torn apart like delicate tissue paper by the maddened prisoners, her last thought was that her sister had been right.

Shikhar Dixit is a New Jersey based writer/illustrator whose work has sold to and appeared in such venues as Barnes & Noble's 100 Crafty Cat Crimes, Barnes & Noble's 365 Scary Stories, Fantastic Stories of the Imagination, E-Scape, Not One of Us, Dark Regions, Gothic.Net, Dr. Casey's Tales From the Internet, Space & Time Magazine, The Darker Side Anthology, Fangoria Online, Horror-Find and Extremes: Horror and Fantasy From the Ends of the Earth. He is an active member of the GSHW and the HWA. Shikhar resides in the darkest heart of New Jersey with his wife and his carnivorous plant, Veruca Salt.

Bev O'Neill lives in Sandusky, Ohio, with her white Angora cat "April." Her genre and slipstream pieces have started to appear in the last year or so in Cyberthirst, Glyph, Whispers from the Shattered Forum, Delirium, Alternate Realities, and Speculon.

"The authors who most influence me are those who take unfamiliar realities and make them plausible, who knock the rose-colored glasses off my face and shove my nose in it—"it" being the fiction: Michele Tea's frantic survival, Johanna Lindsey's submissive, adolescent sexual fantasies, George R.R. Martin's blatant human evil and ambition, David Drake's comprehension of when push comes to shove. I try to reach into my own imagination and twist what couldn't be—or could if it can be conceived. Listen . . ."

Erik Johnson dropped out of graduate school for writing and hopes you can tell. His work has appeared in New York Stories, The Absinthe Literary Review, and The Midnighter's Club Anthology, among other publications. He has just finished his first novel, a fantasy about Mr. Sunday the living skeleton, and is currently working on a second unrelated book. Erik proudly lives in New York with two cats and an obscenely large CD collection.

"The Racists" was written as both a straight horror tale and a darkly humorous take on language and how it shapes our perceptions in America.

Jason Brannon cut his literary teeth on Spider-Man comics, Ray Bradbury short stories, and Richard Laymon novels. His stories have appeared in over 80 publications including Twilight Showcase, Electric Wine, The Edge: Tales of Suspense, Bloody Muse, Dark Realms, Peridot Books, Welcome to Nod, Horrorfind.com and Black Petals. His debut novel, Rusty Nails, will be published in the late spring by The Fiction Works and a new short story collection, Five Days on the Banks of the Acheron, will be out from Double Dragon Books before year's end. He also has work scheduled to appear in The Dead Inn, Vol 2 from Delirium Books, the Hour of Pain anthology, and Rogue Worlds. When not writing or attending to his duties as editor of The Haunted webzine, Jason can sometimes be found lurking in one of the dark corners of his webpage at http://www.angelfire.com/rant/puzzles/

Though she recently betrayed her Gothic roots by begining to wear colors, **Gemma Files** still often invites all and sundry to, as poet Susan Musgrave puts it, "bite into [her]/ and open [their] mind to blood." She is a freelance film critic and a screenwriting/Canadian Film History teacher, and has adapted two of her own works for Showtime's THE HUNGER; her short story "The Emperor's Old Bones" won an International Horror Writers' Guild award for Best Short Story of 1999. Her latest chapbooks, HEART'S HOLE and NARUKH: CHAOS ENGINE, are currently available for order online at http://members.tripod.com/gemma_files/.

Darren Speegle resides with his family in Rhineland, Germany, where he has been guilty of mooching off the setting for many of his tales. He is the author of some fifty published stories, his work having appeared in the publications REDSINE, CHIAROSCURO, WRITER ONLINE, FORTEAN BUREAU, BLOODFETISH and RECKLESS ABANDON, to name a few. Look for future tales in the anthologies FRESH BLOOD, OF FLESH AND HUNGER and DARKNESS RISING. His collection That Old World Gothic was released in August 2001 by Renaissance E Books. "Lagniappe" was recently published in chapbook form by Anxiety Pubs. Visit Darren's website at http://www.geocities.com/koobie2stoobies.

"In "Along the Footpath to Oblivion," a wrench is thrown into the routine of pair of murderous waylayers."

Steven A. Roman made his professional writing debut in 1993 with the publication of his comic book horror series Lorelei. Outside the comics industry, Roman was a contributor to the prose anthologies Untold Tales of Spider-Man and The Ultimate Hulk, and was the editor of the ibooks, inc. novels Heavy Metal: F.A.K.K.2, Moebius' Arzach, The Alien Factor (by X-Men co-creator Stan Lee), and, yes, even Britney Spears is a Three-Headed Alien. Currently, he's working on Book 3 of The Chaos Engine, and a summer 2002 re-launch of Lorelei. He lives in Queens, New York.

Michael Laimo's first novel ATMOSPHERE will be out from Leisure Books in Spetember of 2002. His newest collection, DREGS OF SOCIETY, is now available from PRIME. His first collection, DEMONS, FREAKS, AND OTHER ABNORMALITIES will be reissued in trade paperback this year from Delirium Books. He lives in Melville NY with Sherrie, Anna, and Puddy.

"In my failed search to unearth pictures of human oddities on the internet, I wrote the following story about the website I'd hoped to find."

Loren MacLeod now resides in Virginia, but while

attending Columbia University she lived on Claremont Avenue between 124th and 125th Streets. There was a crackhouse/brothel down the block, and a park around the corner where once in a while someone was shot or knifed to death. Such features made it an interesting neighborhood that partially inspired the setting for this story. Other works by the author have appeared this year in Wet: More Aqua Erotica; Dead But Dreaming: New Excursions into the Lovecraftian Universe; Fresh Blood: New Wounds on the Body of Horror; and in the zine Black Petals. She is also a nominee for the 2001 British Fantasy Award in the short fiction section.

Mark McLaughlin occasionally stops writing long enough to eat, bathe and sometimes even sleep (though not too much of that last one). He wrote one-third of a big new book of dark poetry, The Gossamer Eye—the other poets contained therein are Rain Graves and David Niall Wilson. Mark has a solo poetry collection coming out later this year entitled Professor LaGungo's Exotic Artifacts & Assorted Mystic Collectibles. And, next year he has two hardback story collections coming out—Slime After Slime and Hell Is Where The Heart Is.

"I think it is sad that people often dislike others because they are 'different' or 'weird'. After all, 'different' just means that the other person has walked paths less traveled —and so, who is to say which paths are the best?"

Cathy Buburuz, formerly a communications specialist with the Canadian federal government, now serves as the editor of Champagne Shivers Magazine and the Side Show anthology. Watch for her horror story "Desiderada" in City Slab, and do check out her many contributions to Erin Donahoe's soon to be published Modern Art Cave anthology. "Buburuz" is the Romanian word for "Ladybug."

Canadian writer Cathy Buburuz contributed "Beyond Ledra" to "Underworlds," a nasty little tale about a Cajun serial killer on a guilt trip.

Christopher Stires has had over forty-five short stories accepted by publications such as Fangoria, Fantastic: Stories of the Imagination, The Edge: Tales of Suspense, Vestal Review, Outer Darkness, Hardboiled, Whispers from the Shattered Forum, Redsine (Australia), DarkMoon (UK), and others. His dark fantasy novel, The Inheritance, is currently available in eBook format at The Fiction Works (www.fictionworks.com) and will soon will available in trade paperback from Zumaya Publications (www.zumayapublications.com). Soon he will have stories appearing in Darkness Rising 7: Demons at Play, The Best of Pirate Writings II, Deathly Desires, Crux, Dramatourges of the Yann (Greece), and others. Christopher lives in Southern California with his wife, Annie, and daughter, Katie.

Jack Fisher has been writing dark fantasy fiction for over five years. He's sold his work to the likes of Cemetery Dance, Space & Time, Dark Regions, Black October, The Urbanite, Redsine, Not One of Us, and many more. Jack edits the multi award-winning (Writer's Digest, Jobs in Hell) magazine, Flesh & Blood (www.fleshandbloodpress.com). Jack is a paramedic in central New Jersey. He's currently attending school to become an RN.

Karen Carpenter has written over thirty horror stories and recently compiled a collection of her favorites. She has also written numerous picture books for children and two novellas for young adults. The New York Vietnam Veterans Memorial Commission used Karen's stark photograph of a soldier's tombstone in its advertising campaign—which helped raise over three million dollars for the Memorial in lower Manhattan. Monthly, Karen writes a column, "Staying Connected" for The Graveline—the official newsletter of "The Garden State Horror Writers". She is currently at work on a novel, "Hans", a spine tingling, supernatural thriller. Look for her stories "Survival" at Apocalypse Fiction, "Must Be True Love" in the upcoming anthology In A Fearful State and "Victims" in an upcoming edition of Whispers From the Shattered Forum. She lives in New Jersey with her sweet, mild-mannered husband, Charlie, and their boundlessly exuberant black lab, Buddy.

On writing "Eloise": "While perusing Internet sites of haunted places, I couldn't help but wonder what might make a man sit alone in his van at night, staring silently into the ruins of this old asylum . . ."

Nicholas Knight's stories can be found in anthologies such as Sideshow, The Hour of Pain, The Midnighters Club, The Witching Hour, and The Rhine Research Center's Parapsychological Mysteries, as well as magazines such as Whispers From the Shattered Forum, Futures Mysterious Anthology, Black Petals, and Alternate Realities. He can be contacted at knight@darktales.zzn.com

About "Life's Loser": A man's successes in life are undermined by the constant one-upmanship of a perpetual antagonist, until his anger reaches the breaking point. I wrote the story after observing a number of so-called friendships wherein one friend always felt the need to put down the other in order to appear superior.

Derrick M. Hussey has been a reader of horror since his teens, and since 1997 has been writing for the Esoteric Order of Dagon amateur press association. He is founder and editor of Hippocampus Press (www.hippocampuspress.com), which publishes Clark Ashton Smith, H. P. Lovecraft and others.

"This is a revised version of an article that originally appeared in Derrick's EOD journal Amethystine Hippocampus."

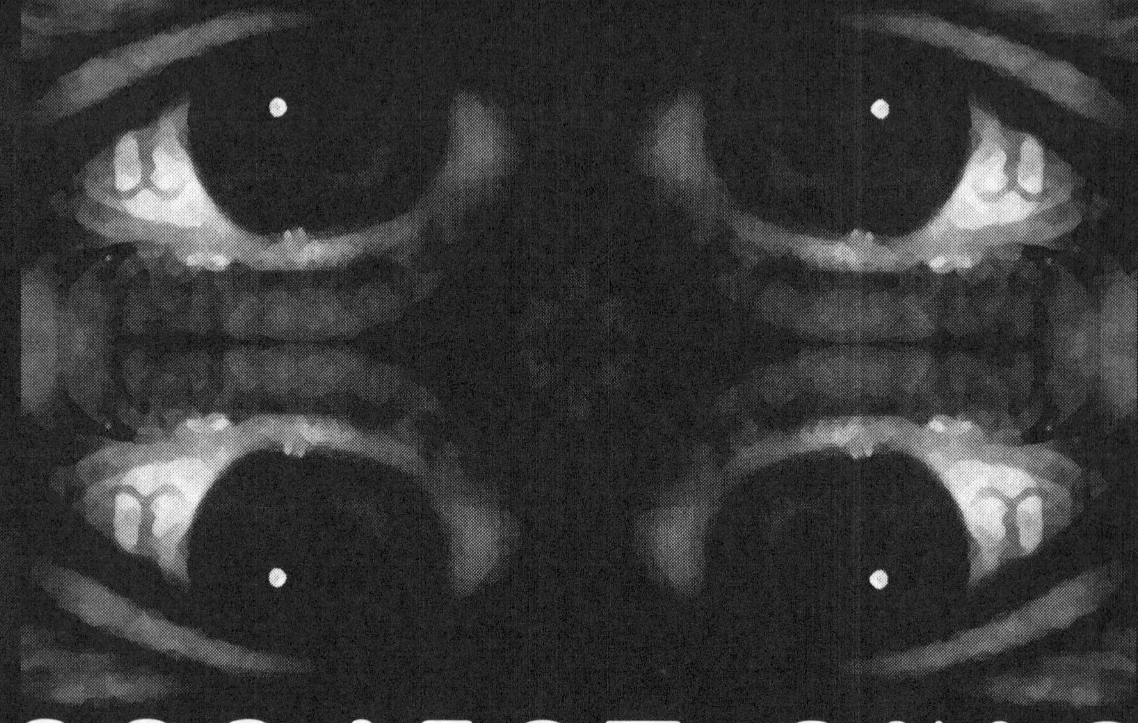
the dot com of the small press

PROJECT PULP

"we mean business"

WWW.PROJECTPULP.COM

BOOKS & MAGAZINES   HORROR   SCIENCE FICTION   FANTASY   MYSTERY/SUSPENSE
LITERARY   POETRY   EROTICA/ROMANCE   NON-FICTION   CDS   and much more!

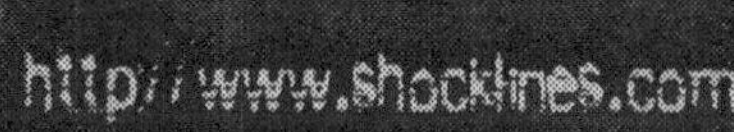

SHOCKLINES.COM
Shock.
www.shocklines.com
You've never seen
a bookstore like this
http://www.shocklines.com
CANIGLIA